REACHING JESUS

Five Steps to a Fuller Life

David Knight

ST. ANTHONY MESSENGER PRESS

Cincinnati, Ohio

Nihil Obstat: Rev. Arthur J. Espelage, O.F.M.
Rev. Robert L. Hagedorn

Imprimi Potest: Rev. John Bok, O.F.M.
Provincial

Imprimatur: +Most Reverend Carl K. Moeddel, V.G.
Archdiocese of Cincinnati
March 3, 1997

Cover design by Karla Ann Sheppard
Cover photograph by Gene Plaisted, O.S.C.
Electronic pagination and format design by Sandy L. Digman

ISBN 0-86716-296-1

Published by St. Anthony Messenger Press
Printed in the U.S.A.

Contents

—————————◼—————————

INTRODUCTION

———————■———————

Five Steps Into the Fullness of Life

This book is about five things you need to do in order to enter into the experience of Jesus Christ as savior, teacher, leader, lover and lord. In the experience of union with him on these levels you will discover the fullness of the life of grace.

Everyone desires "life to the full"—a full life, a meaningful life, a productive life, a happy life. However we understand and define these things, they are what our hearts desire.

Jesus of Nazareth defined himself as being the life

that all people seek, as well as being the way to it. "I am the way and the truth and the life," he said (John 14:6). His reason for coming into the world was that we might "have life and have it to the full" (see John 10:10). The decision whether or not to believe that Jesus is the life we seek is the most important decision we will ever make, because it sets the course of our lives.

It is not enough just to affirm in words or accept intellectually that Jesus is the savior of the world. If we really believe that the fullness of life we long for is found in union with Jesus, we will direct our whole lives toward acquiring that union. If we really believe Jesus is the way to the fullness of life, we will follow him; we will base everything we do on his words and example.

For two thousand years Christians have proclaimed Jesus of Nazareth to be the "Christ"—the "Anointed One." But for each of us those two thousand years of belief are not as important as the one moment in our own life in which we make the decision to accept Jesus as the Messiah, the Anointed One, and to direct our lives toward him as our fulfillment.

Actually, this is not a single moment of decision; it is a recurring moment, a decision made and persevered in, a commitment. Commitments are the most important acts of our lives; they give shape to our souls.

Every decision, every free choice, is an act of self-determination. Our free choices create us as the persons we will be for all eternity. In free choices we experience most deeply what it is to be human, to be in the image of God. With every free choice we say, "Let it be!"—and it is. In free choices we choose to believe, to love, to hate; we choose to live life to the full or to turn away from life in its fullness. In these moments of freedom we create ourselves as believers, as lovers or haters, as people of hope or despair.

A commitment is a moment of freedom that endures. Free choices are words that are spoken; commitments are words that are sung. In commitments we hold the note; the choice continues, our moment of freedom is prolonged. Our commitments—the truths we choose to believe, the ideals we choose to embrace, the directions we choose to take, the goals we choose to pursue, the hopes we choose to live by—these are the enduring choices that shape our souls, make us the persons we are and determine the true meaning of our names.

Jesus Christ invites us to create ourselves, to shape our souls, by the response we make to him. This choice, this enduring decision, is the most important commitment of our lives. In fact, if we understand it as including all the particular commitments that follow from it or are included in it, it is the only commitment that counts. All other choices and commitments in life have no permanent significance, no enduring value, except insofar as in one way or another they are acts of response to the person and the message of Jesus Christ.

Whether people respond to Jesus consciously, knowing his name, or whether, like the wise men from the East in Matthew's Gospel, they respond to him by following the star through which God speaks to them, there is no other way that leads to life except the way that leads to Jesus. He, and he alone, is the way, the truth and the life.

The purpose of this book is simply to mark that path, so that those who choose to follow it will know where they are, will understand what steps they have already taken, and what steps they need to take next in order to reach Christ, to arrive at that union with him in which the fullness of life is found.

This book is about five choices, five commitments, that are essential to our commitment to follow Jesus Christ. They are the five basic choices we have to make in order to live the life Jesus came to give in abundance: the life of grace. A whole, integral Christian life requires these five commitments. They lead to the total gift of ourselves in love.

Implicit in these five commitments to life in Christ are five choices to die, five graves into which we must enter in order to rise to the fullness of life.

Does this sound frightening? It shouldn't. Jesus taught, "Those who want to save their life will lose it, and those who lose their life for my sake will find it" (see Matthew 10:39). Jesus accepted death for himself as the way to multiply his life on earth: "Unless a grain of wheat falls to the ground and dies, it remains just a grain of wheat; but if it dies, it produces much fruit" (John 12:24).

Saint Paul reminds us that our Baptism was a dying and a rising: "[A]re you unaware that we who were baptized into Christ Jesus were baptized into his death? We were indeed buried with him through baptism into death, so that, just as Christ was raised from the dead by the glory of the Father, we too might live in newness of life" (Romans 6:3-4).

The Christian life is a constant dying to what is less in order to live what is more. "[W]e who live are constantly being given up to death for the sake of Jesus, so that the life of Jesus may be manifested in our mortal flesh" (2 Corinthians 4:11). These "deaths" are not loss for us, but gain: "For if you live according to the flesh, you will die, but if by the spirit you put to death the deeds of the body, you will live" (Romans 8:13)—and live life to the full. Saint Paul is not talking only about accepting physical death in exchange for eternal life in heaven; he is talking about dying to anything and everything that diminishes our response to Jesus Christ on earth so that we might begin to experience the fullness of life here and now.

To arrive at fullness of life we need to enter into and rise out of five graves. We need to speak five words of life; by each of them we die to something less, something diminished, and rise to something more.

Five graves, five risings: That is the substance of this book. Baptism committed us to all of them. But it is possible, even probable, that neither at the time of our Baptism nor afterward did we ever put them specifically in focus. We are committed to them all; we are even living them all in a general, perhaps haphazard, way. And they are bearing fruit in our lives. But perhaps not the fruit they ought to bear, and not the fruit they can bear if we live them to the full.

The Christian life, the life of grace, is meant to be an ongoing experience of passionate living on every level: body, emotions, mind and will. The Christian life, passionately lived in love, is meant to give us life to the full, joy to the full.

It is meant to be an experience of God, an experience of Christ, an experience of being Christ, of being his body, seeing with his eyes, choosing according to the desires of his heart, living by his divine life, giving his life to others. It is an experience of redeeming the world.

At Baptism each of us was anointed with chrism and consecrated by God to carry on the mission of Jesus. Each one of us was sealed and committed, consecrated and anointed to be prophet, priest and steward of Christ's kingship. We were christened, "Christ-ed," so that we might continue the life and mission of the Anointed One on earth, so that we might be Christ.

"Let us rejoice and give thanks," Saint Augustine says to the baptized, "for we have become not only Christians, but Christ.... Marvel and rejoice: we have become Christ!"[1]

To "be Christ" and to experience our union with him, to live out our baptismal anointing with clear and conscious awareness, is to live life to the full. But for this we need to understand clearly each commitment included in that anointing. We need to accept it explicitly, and try specifically to live it out in action.

This book is a guide to these five choices to die to ourselves and rise to being Christ. It offers five steps into the fullness of life. The five choices are simple. They are clear and specific. And they are all easy, at least at the beginning. They can lead to "heroic living of the Gospel" (the formula for canonization!), but you don't have to be heroic to start living them. You don't even have to be an especially good Christian. You just have to be willing to start.

It is sort of like jogging: the more you do, the more you become able to do. So let's begin.

Notes

[1] This is the teaching of John Paul II, quoting Saint Augustine: "Having become one with Christ, the Christian 'becomes a member of his Body, which is the Church' (cf. 1 Cor 12:13, 27). By the work of the Spirit, Baptism radically configures the faithful to Christ in the Paschal Mystery of death and resurrection; it 'clothes him' in Christ (cf. Gal 3:27): 'Let us rejoice and give thanks,' exclaims Saint Augustine speaking to the baptized, 'for we have become not only Christians, but Christ... Marvel and rejoice: we have become Christ!'" *The Splendor of Truth*, Chapter One, #21 (Boston: St. Paul Books and Media, 1993).

STEP ONE

---■---

The Choice to Be a Christian

Dying to False Hopes and Saviors;
Rising to Jesus Christ, Savior of the World

The first step is the choice to make Jesus Christ as savior an active participant in everything I do. This is what it means to be a Christian. To do this I have to die to all trust in my ability to save any part of my life in this world without giving Jesus an active part. This is the first grave.

The first step will transform our whole life, but it is not difficult, nor is it vague or complicated. It is a simple—but profound—decision to do something practical and concrete.

As Christians we believe that Jesus Christ is alive, that he is present to us all the time, that he sees our every action and hears our every word. More than that, we believe he is present within us, that he lives in us by grace, sharing his divine life with us, sharing in our human lives and in all our human actions.

Whether we think about it or not, and whether we explicitly choose it or not, as long as we are united to God by grace, Jesus has an active part in everything we do. There is not a word we speak, not a thought we have or choice we make that Jesus does not want to influence—or doesn't try to influence, in the measure that we leave ourselves open to his action.

But he will not violate our freedom, and he will not force his influence upon us. His union with us by grace is a partnership—for him to act with us we have to act freely with him. Every graced choice and action has to be a joint decision. If we don't choose to act in partnership with him, we put up an obstacle to his acting in partnership with us.

The first step along the path to the fullness of life is to make a conscious act of faith that Jesus Christ is living within us, and to invite him to take part in every thought, word, action and decision of our life.

You might pause to do this right now.

Then we have to show that we mean it. We have to try consciously to make Jesus Christ an active participant in everything we do. We need to interact consciously with him in every activity of our day.

This sounds simple, and it is. It is also concrete and

down-to-earth. There is no one who cannot do it. So why is it that so many people don't? The answer—for many, at least—is that they don't realize the need. Most people don't consult a doctor until they feel sick. Most people don't ask for advice until they feel confused. And most Christians, it would seem, do not interact with Jesus as savior all day, every day, simply because they don't think such constant interaction with him is necessary for salvation. For them, to say "Jesus is savior" means that Jesus has opened the gates of heaven for us. It does not mean that Jesus has to be the foundation of our lives here and now.

So what does it take to accept Jesus Christ authentically as the only savior of the world?

A Prerequisite

Before we can build our lives solidly on Jesus Christ as a foundation, we have to dig a hole. The deeper the hole, the stronger the foundation. This means we have to go deeply into ourselves and understand our need for Jesus. We have to be deeply convinced that Jesus Christ is not an option, that seeking total relationship with him is not an "extra." Only a relationship with Jesus can save us from veering off into destructiveness, distortion, mediocrity and meaninglessness.

If we think the choice before us is just a choice to be more rather than less—more Christian, more holy, more religious, more devout—we don't understand the question. It is not a question of more or less; it is a question of either-or.

The question is, "Do you believe that Jesus Christ is the only savior of the world, the only one who can save your life right now from becoming what you really don't want it to be?" This means your personal relationships and family life, your social life, your professional life. You need to understand this invitation as an either-or: Either make Jesus an effective, operative part of everything you do, or see your life "miss the mark" (the root meaning of *sin*) and slide off into destructiveness, distortion, mediocrity and meaninglessness.

The Root of the Problem: Original Sin

Why do we need to be so pessimistic? Aren't we all basically good people? Isn't our society founded on good principles and values? Isn't what we have learned from our religion enough? Aren't the Ten Commandments sufficient to keep us on course and living reasonably good lives? Why do we have to relate consciously to Jesus, to interact explicitly with Jesus in everything we do?

The answer lies in the concept of original sin. Yes, people are basically good. God did not give us flawed equipment; our human natures were not made defective at the factory. Nor did the sin of Adam jog God's creative hand and cause it to slip. So far as God's work is concerned, we were made perfectly according to specifications.

But beginning with the first sin ever committed on earth, the human environment changed. Because everyone born into the human race must grow up in a formative society, in a culture, when the human environment changed, the existential situation of every person born into this world was altered at the root.

We are social beings. The family, the society, the culture into which we are born radically influence our attitudes, values and behavior. Before we are old enough to understand what we are doing or to make free choices we are already being programmed by our environment to feel, to think and to act in particular ways, both good and bad. The world into which we are born shapes our initial attitudes, values, priorities and patterns of behavior in ways too all-pervasive to analyze. Absolutely no one is exempt from its influence. Once sin came into the world, the good influences of culture were intermingled with bad influences.

Original Sin—and the cumulative effect of every free human choice, from the first sin to the most recent one—has injected falsehood or distortion into the environment. The world was not created bad; people were not created bad; but the environment into which all people are born was created and is being created now as both good and bad by the free actions of individual human beings. For centuries upon centuries these free actions have been both good and bad. The human environment has been enhanced by the good actions of people and infected by their bad actions, and this is the environment that forms and shapes the fears and desires, the assumptions and prejudices, the emotions and perceptions of every human being born into the world.

Because of the distortion of truth in the environment, our intellects are darkened. Because of the distortion of values in the environment our wills are weakened by fears and misdirected desires. This is a characteristic of our being, of human existence on earth. From the moment we are conceived in our mother's womb we exist in solidarity with the human race and are subject to its influence.

This, in part at least, is the meaning of Original Sin. And this is why we are doomed to live and act in ways that are distorted and destructive unless we are re-formed, re-shaped and re-created in our perceptions and judgments, in our attitudes and values by Jesus Christ, the only true light of the world. Only Jesus can show us without distortion the way to live and the truth by which to live; only Jesus can lead us to life. That is why he said, "I am the way and the truth and the life. No one comes to the Father except through me" (John 14:6).

Only through constant, daily interaction with Jesus as master of the way and teacher of life can we gradually be freed from the darkness and distortions of our culture, purify our values and desires, put aside the fears and priorities programmed into us by our culture and learn to live life to the full. To seek this ongoing, constant interaction with Jesus as the way, the truth and the life is what it means to accept Jesus as savior.

What Is Ground Level?

"Being saved" doesn't mean just getting to heaven, any more than "being holy" means just keeping out of sin. Being saved means entering fully into life. We can be more or less saved, just as we can be more or less alive. Like the young man in the Gospel who had kept the commandments all his life, we need to ask Jesus, "What do I still lack?"

Christians recognize that they need Jesus to get to heaven, and most of us pray for his help against the temptations and sins we recognize. But we do not pray for help against what we perceive as normal behavior. Once we have achieved a certain measure of control over our lives, enough to be accepted as mature, self-disciplined adults who live the way everyone expects us to live, we may not consciously feel any daily need for Jesus. We may think we are doing well enough so long as we are not doing anything we recognize as positively wrong.

But are we really able to recognize what is wrong, given the distorted attitudes and values we grew up with? Did our ancestors recognize slavery as wrong? What about segregation? Going back in time, did Christians see that it was wrong to burn one another at the stake over differences in belief? To use the sword to force whole nations to their knees before the cross?

And if what we are doing is in fact good, how good is "good enough" for someone who shares in the life of God, who is called to live on God's level? Jesus called his disciples the "salt of the earth" and the "light of the world." Until we stand out as such in the ordinary, daily actions of our life we are not fully saved.

We need to be awakened to see what we really need to be saved from. We can live for years not appreciating the real power of sin in our lives, not knowing what our most destructive sins are—or even that we have any. Without deep interaction with Jesus Christ, we accept many evils as good, just because everyone else does.

Unless we measure ourselves constantly by the example and ideals of Jesus himself, we will unconsciously accept the common denominator of our society's standards. In doing this we fall into the complacent belief that even though we may not be perfect, we are, for all practical purposes, living perfectly good lives.

We need Jesus as savior in order to recognize the difference between darkness, semidarkness and light.

If we are to have any hope of persevering in our commitment, then before we can decide to make Jesus an active, redeeming participant in our lives, we need to dig down into our hearts, to go deep in self-knowledge and to lay a foundation of life-giving despair. We need to see and feel deeply the truth of this statement: Unless we give Jesus Christ an active role in our lives, everything we do will veer off into destructiveness, distortion, mediocrity and meaninglessness.

Going Beneath the Surface

Some of us know by experience how this slide into darkness begins. We have seen marriages begin beautifully and end ugly. We have seen ourselves doing destructive things to others and to ourselves—at work, in our social lives, as citizens, even as priests or laity engaged in ministry. Without the involvement of Jesus in every area of our lives, anything we do is prone to slide into destructiveness.

Even where our lives have not been destructive we nonetheless recognize distortion. We realize that many of the attitudes and viewpoints we learned from our culture are out of focus. We see that our family life, while perhaps not destructive, is still not perfectly in balance. We recognize a wrong set of priorities in our work, an attitude in our social circle that is not right.

And even where our attitudes and values are not clearly distorted, we sometimes sense a mediocrity in our lives that tells us that something must be wrong. Our marriage is good, but not as good as it could be, not the fulfillment of our dreams. Our work doesn't leave us satisfied at the end of the day. Our social life is flat and superficial. Even religion doesn't give us the peace, the joy we long for. We are leading good but unsatisfying lives, an ordinary existence. We don't taste the "fruit of the Holy Spirit"—love, joy and peace—in everything we do. We are not experiencing the "life to the full" that Jesus came to give.

Finally, there is the specter of meaninglessness, the question that increasingly hangs over our heads in the morning as we get up to begin another day: "What is it all about? Is it worth it? Is this what I want to do with my life?" Even though we know that our lives come from God and lead to ultimate fulfillment in heaven, and even though at times we experience ourselves doing wonderful things for others or for God, we sometimes wonder doubtfully about the long stretches in between.

We can't really appreciate Jesus as Savior—not as the Savior he came to be—until we are deeply convinced that we need to give Jesus Christ an active part in everything we do. Until we do so, our lives here on this earth cannot be saved from destructiveness and distortion, from mediocrity and meaninglessness.

An Act of Life-giving Despair

In order to give our lives over to Jesus Christ, we need to make an act of life-giving despair. We despair of all false messiahs, of anything and everything (except Jesus Christ) that promises to save the meaning and value of our lives on earth. False saviors are false gods. To trust in false gods is idolatry, a violation of the First Commandment: "I am the Lord your God. You shall not have other gods alongside of me" (see Exodus 20:2-3).

This is the first grave we have to enter before we can rise and live. We have to look into our hearts and die to all hope for a full and meaningful life based on confidence in ourselves. We have to look at our daily existence and die to all uncritical trust in the way of living we were taught. We have to give up the security we seek through conformity to our culture. We have to stop relying on the use of our talents and education, on the ultimate healing power of techniques and support groups, on the love of spouse and children, on acceptance by other people, on rewarding dedication to human service and success.

To despair of finding satisfaction, peace, happiness and fulfillment through anything other than Jesus Christ is an act of life-giving despair. It preserves us from false saviors, false messiahs, false gods, and opens us to hope in Jesus as savior.

The Act of Faith in Jesus as Savior

Despair is not enough. What saves us is placing positive faith and hope in Jesus Christ. We despair of false messiahs in order to turn to Jesus with our hope focused only on him. We acknowledge him with deep, personal faith as the "only name under heaven given to the human race by which we are to be saved." This is the act of life-giving hope. It is not to be taken for granted.

Anyone who is Christian professes that Jesus is the "savior of the world." But for many this just means in practice that we depend on Jesus to get us to heaven. How many Christians depend positively on Jesus for fulfillment in their family and social lives, in business and politics? How many show this dependence in real, practical and observable ways? How many really believe that interaction with Jesus Christ can save

these areas of their life from destructiveness and distortion, from mediocrity and meaninglessness? How
many turn to him with real belief when a situation
seems hopeless?

When a marriage is breaking up, how many of us
really believe that combined interaction with Jesus
Christ can save it? This doesn't mean just begging him
in prayer to intervene; it means turning to him as a
couple united in faith and interacting with him, using
every means he has made available to us—praying
and reflecting on Scripture together; using the
Sacrament of Reconciliation with an unconditional
commitment to change anything in our lives that is an
obstacle to love; participating in Mass together, even
daily if that is necessary and possible—and combining
all of this with marriage counseling, group therapy or
any other human help that is called for.

How many believe that interaction with Jesus
Christ can change a nasty situation at work, can transform our working environment—or at least transform
it for ourselves? How many believe that interaction
with Jesus Christ can turn a bad relationship with
someone into a good one? Or change our attitude
toward ourselves? Or put our whole experience of life
on a new, joyous and fulfilling level?

To believe this—and act on it—is to believe in
Jesus as savior. If we only believe that Jesus can get us
to heaven, but not that he can transform our enjoy-
ment of life on earth, then we only believe in him as
the savior of our souls, not as the savior of all we are.
It isn't enough. It doesn't do him justice. Jesus didn't

come just to save our souls; he came to save us, to save everything about us, everything we do, everything we are.

Getting Practical: How Do We Do This?

To give Jesus an active part in everything we do, awareness is half the game. Jesus doesn't break in on our senses like other people do. He doesn't assail our eyes everywhere we look, like advertisements on a city street. He doesn't pound on our ears like TV commercials or the neighbor's radio we don't want to hear. If we want to be conscious of Jesus, we have to provide our own sensory reminders.

First, we can program ourselves to remember. We can form the habit of reminding ourselves each morning when we wake up, "I want to give Jesus an active part in what I do today." Every time we go to work or drive anywhere, we can think of how we might involve Jesus in what we are about to do, or of how he would do it. And while driving back home from work we can think back on how we were or were not conscious of him during the day, and of what difference it made. Before going to sleep we can glance back over the whole day and ask the same question. If we keep doing this, we will grow into an abiding awareness of him that will underlie our consciousness all day long.

If human beings have created an environment that ignores the presence of God, we can structure things into our own environment that remind us of God.

Some people set their watches to beep every hour

as a reminder to remember God's presence. Some put a picture on their desk or at their worksite. Others keep some symbol before their eyes whose meaning is known only to them. Some get into the habit of thinking of Jesus every time they go through a door, start their car or pick up the phone. Until you form the habit you can hang something on the doorknob or on your car keys, or keep something draped over the phone. Some play religious songs as background music while they work. Some, when they are at home, light a candle in the room. Some make the reminder a part of their clothes or jewelry.

You might use some gesture or body language that speaks to you but that no one else would notice: keeping your hand casually on your heart or your finger on your lips while you listen to someone speaking. And, noticeably or not, you can bow your head every time someone around you uses the name of God disrespectfully or insults another person. Whenever anyone's language shows a lack of appreciation for what is sacred you can consciously hear that with Jesus and be aware of how he feels about it.

Our senses belong to us. We can't control much of what other people force on our eyes or ears, but we can counterbalance the images, words and sounds that are part of our environment with others of our own making. We can give Jesus equal time on the airwaves. Whenever a commercial comes on, for example, you can remember Jesus and say a prayer—or comment to him about what you have just seen on the news or in a program.

Is this practical enough? Down-to-earth enough? Can you make a decision to put it into practice? What will you start with?

The Channels of Interaction

Just being aware of Jesus is not enough; we need to interact with him as we do with friends. And we can do this in several ways, on a number of different levels.

Rinky-dink Prayers. One way is to make constant use of "rinky-dink" prayer. A rinky-dink prayer is a prayer for something that is not important enough to bother the Almighty about. When we make it, we become conscious that Jesus is our friend.

I discovered rinky-dink prayer one evening when I was putting a roof on a carport. I was pressing to finish before dark, and in my haste I kept dropping roofing tacks onto the driveway where I knew they would lie waiting for my car tires. I noticed that each time I dropped a tack and scrambled down the ladder in the increasing darkness to look for it, I would start to say a prayer: "Lord, help me find that tack!"

And it irked me. My spontaneous reaction to making the prayer was irritation. I felt humiliated, degraded in some way because I was asking God for help to do what I was perfectly capable of doing myself. In an attempt to justify my irritation, I told myself, "If my best friend were president of the United States I wouldn't call him up to fix a parking ticket." And then the thought came to me, "No, but if my best friend were standing at the bottom of this ladder, the first thing I would do when I dropped a tack would be to yell down, 'Hey, did you see where that tack went?'"

I got the point. To treat Jesus as a friend instead of just as God is to let him be a friend—and this is one way to grow in awareness of him as friend. Now I pray to him constantly, asking him to do anything I would ask a friend to do: "Lord, find me a parking place." "Show me a good restaurant." "Don't let me blow it on this phone call."

Most rinky-dink prayers don't call for the use of overwhelming divine power—maybe for just a little bit, like, "Lord, keep the light green till I get there." But if we know that Jesus is our friend, we do ask him also for serious things—and then we ask him seriously. Then it is not rinky-dink prayer; it is the prayer of petition. Or if it is for other people, it is called intercessory prayer.

Prayers of Petition. I don't have access to many powerful people. I can hardly get in to see my doctor sometimes, much less the movers and shakers of business and politics. But I have instant access to the savior of the world, any time, any place. All of us do, as often as we want, for as long as we desire. There is no concern in our lives that we cannot present personally to Jesus Christ. And when we do, we are sure that we will be listened to with attention and with love. To go to Jesus with our petitions is a way of interacting with him that helps keep us aware of who he is for us and what he wants to be.

One of the early Jesuits, Blessed Peter Faber, used to look out the window when he was traveling and pray for the workers he saw in the fields, for children playing in the streets, for the occupants of a house that looked peaceful—or a house that did not. We can pray for the drivers on the freeway who annoy us, for the business people we deal with, for the situations we see on the news, for our family, friends and enemies. We can pray for better housing when we drive through poor neighborhoods, and when we drive through affluent neighborhoods we can pray that all who live there will find peace in following the values and example of Jesus.

Prayers of Consultation and Desire. One of the most important ways of interacting with Jesus is to make him a part of every decision and action of our lives by consulting him beforehand. We don't have to spend a great deal of time consulting him—unless we are making an important decision that calls for much prayerful reflection. But we should not make any decision without at least passing it by Jesus, asking him for guidance and asking ourselves what we believe he thinks about it.

People who work with others as a team do this constantly. Partners consult each other. So do married couples. When we don't have time to talk over a decision, we at least ask ourselves mentally what the other would think of it. And we who are coworkers with Jesus Christ became part of his body at Baptism, consecrated and committed to bearing witness to him through every detail of our life-style. If we are trying to advance the reign of God through everything we are involved in, should we not consult him before every decision we make?

This is a key way to make Jesus Christ an active participant in everything we do. We may not always know what decision he would make; we may not always have the courage or the love to do what we know he would do. But just to consult him with good will is already to give him an active role that will gradually transform our lives.

The Prayer Beyond Prayers. The most powerful way to make Jesus a part of everything we do is to participate daily in the mystery of the Mass. For some people this may be impossible because they are restricted in space or time—homebound, for example, or tied to inflexible schedules. But if all those who actually could were to free themselves to offer Jesus Christ daily at Mass for the redemption of their world, the churches would not be able to contain them.

At Mass Jesus on the cross is made present in our space and time, offering himself as he did on Calvary. We who know this can be there, united to him, one with him as members of his body. We can offer this sacrifice for the sin and suffering we ourselves are aware of, for the needs of the world we will walk in that day. There is no better way to grow into consciousness of Jesus as savior of the world than to be united with him daily in the mystery of the act by which he redeemed the world.

Rising to Living Life

Jesus said, "I came that they might have life, and have it to the full" (John 10:10). When we have died to all that cannot bring us this fullness of life, we have entered into the first grave.

Entering the grave is the first step toward choosing to rise from the grave and live. We decide deeply, personally and firmly that we really believe in Jesus Christ as the savior of our lives here on earth as well as in heaven. We make a decision, based on despair and hope: despair of everything this world offers as ultimate; hope in everything Jesus promises as immediately available to us now. We decide that we will base our whole lives on relationship with Jesus Christ as savior.

Relationship means interaction. In practice, then, this means that we decide and choose to interact with Jesus Christ in every area of our life—in family and social life, in business and politics; in short, we make Jesus Christ an active participant in everything we do.

Questions for Reflection and Discussion

■ *Is there any area of my life that needs to be saved from destructiveness? Distortion? Meaninglessness? Mediocrity?*

■ *What difference do I think it would make if I consciously interacted with Jesus in this area? In all the areas and actions of my life?*

■ *What concrete and specific actions can I take to give Jesus Christ an active part in everything I do? Where should I begin? How, when, where will I do this?*

STEP TWO

—————— ■ ——————

The Choice to Be a Disciple

Dying to Inadequate Lights and Teachers;
Rising to Discipleship

The second step is the choice to lead a life characterized by reflection on the message of Jesus. This is what
it means to be a disciple. To do this I have to die to
reliance on the goals and guidance of my culture. This
is the second grave.

There are very few disciples of Jesus Christ, even
among Christians. The word *disciple* doesn't mean
"follower," it means "student." To be disciples of Jesus
Christ, we have to be his students; that is, we have to

be studying under him now. Few Christians are doing that.

Unless we are actually (and that means actively) sitting at the feet of Jesus in some way, actively devoting ourselves to learning from him here and now, at this particular period in our lives, we are not his disciples.

We may believe in him. We may be doing what we have already learned. We may be observing all the laws and teachings we have received from him. And we may have been disciples in the past. We may have studied his teaching in grade school or high school, or even have a doctorate in theology. But if we are not in some way sitting at his feet and learning from him here and now, we are not his disciples now. Since no one graduates from the school of Jesus until death, if we are not disciples we are dropouts.

This is what keeps Christians from entering into the fullness of life: We don't choose to be disciples. The choice to be a disciple is a simple, concrete choice. Becoming a disciple of Jesus Christ is not complicated. All you have to do is start learning. All it takes to become a student is to start studying.

A First Step: Get Acquainted With the Bible

This first step can be as simple as the decision to pick up the Bible and begin reading it. You can begin anywhere. I would suggest beginning with the New Testament. Start with the Gospel of Matthew, and then keep going.

What if you don't understand it? Well, if you don't understand it, you will have questions. That is good, because then you can look for answers. And when you get the answers you will have learned something. See how easy it is?

"Yes, but where will I get the answers?" Simple. Call your parish. If the priest is not available, many parishes have others on the staff who are well educated in Scripture and theology. You may have a friend who studies Scripture and would like to share this knowledge with you.

You could also join or form a group to study the Bible. Your parish may be offering Scripture study already; if not, ask if you can start it. Call your diocesan resource center; someone there will know where Bible study groups can be found in your area. When I said there are few disciples of Jesus Christ, even among Christians, I didn't mean there aren't any. And there are more now than there were before Vatican II. All you have to do is ask around, and you will find there are several groups in your town, probably even in your parish, who meet to read and discuss Scripture. You can learn from them.

There are more Protestant groups than Catholic. But if you go to a Protestant group, especially if it calls itself "nondenominational," make sure it is a solid group with a reputation for "respect-ability"; that is, the ability to respect learning and scholarship and the spiritual experience of other denominations. Steer clear of the fundamentalists who ignore—or even condemn—serious scholarship, perhaps in the name of "just sticking to the Bible." Enthusiasts with a simplistic approach to everything can get you excited about reading Scripture. They can get you moving, but so can someone who yells "Fire!" in a movie theater. It's not the most responsible way to generate a response. Enthusiasm without solid direction can be dangerous.

Why don't we understand the Bible? Catholics are quick to say they don't understand the Bible and that they don't know how to pray with Scripture. No one reading this book should ever say that again! Catholics often say they don't understand the Bible because the four passages from Scripture proclaimed at Sunday Mass are the only exposure to it that most Catholics have: usually a reading from the Old Testament, followed by a psalm, then two readings taken from the writings of the apostles and from the Gospels. These are read one after another, with only the briefest pause between them.

No one listening to four short passages lifted out of various books of the Bible and proclaimed one after the other in a ten-minute period can hope to understand anything. It would make as much sense to expect people to walk into a movie theater, watch a single three-minute scene and then walk out and say they "understood" the movie.

The problem is simple: Catholics don't understand the Bible because they have never read it. And they think they can't understand the Bible because when it is read to them at Mass it frequently leaves them confused. The solution is just as simple. Read the Bible. Read each book of the Bible as a book, not as a collection of disconnected sayings. Read the whole Bible as a series of books that keep referring to each other and that cannot be understood completely except in relationship to each other. Once you are familiar with the whole, you will be able to understand the parts.

But this takes time, doesn't it? Yes. It means you have to do some reading, just as you did when you took courses in school. It means that in order to understand what is read at Mass you have to do some homework: Read the readings ahead of time; prepare yourself for what you are going to hear.

Make the choice to be a disciple, to be a student of Jesus Christ. This is a simple choice, a concrete choice. It is not difficult, nor does it cost you anything to pick up the Bible and start reading it. But here is the question: What do you believe you might get out of it?

The Scriptures are the word of God. Does that answer the question?

How to Pray With Scripture

Why do people say they "can't pray" with Scripture? Why do some people say they don't know how to pray, period?

The first reason is because they use the word *pray*. This is a word from ordinary speech that was changed into a religious word. As a result, it has lost its meaning for us. This happens all the time.

The word *disciple*, for example, is not really a religious word. It is just an ordinary word that means "student." But when we made it into a religious word by using it almost exclusively to refer to the disciples of Jesus, we forgot what it meant. So we have Christians who call themselves disciples of Jesus because they believe in him, although they are not students of his at all.

And we have Christians who say they cannot "pray," when as a matter of fact they ask for things all the time—from God as well as from other people. The word *pray*, after all, simply means "to ask."

If a character in a Shakespearian play says, "I pray thee, young maiden, will you come with me?" we have no reason to believe there is anything religious about his intention at all. But when we use the word *pray* we give it a special religious meaning; right away we assume that we don't know how to do it.

So let's not talk about praying with Scripture. Let's talk about things we know we can do, like reading and thinking and choosing. The best definition I can give of "praying with Scripture" is to read a passage from the Bible and think about it until you come to some decision about something you are actually able to do.

Can you read?

"Yes."

Can you think about what you have read?

"Yes, but it doesn't get me anywhere. I go blank."

OK, "to think" is too abstract anyway. Can you ask a bunch of questions about what you read—like, "What does this mean? Who is Jesus talking to? Why does he say this? Why should I do it? How can I? When? Where? For how long? What do I need to do first?" Can you try to answer them?

"Yes, I can do that. But it doesn't turn me on. I don't seem to get any of those great insights you're supposed to get. All my answers seem to lead nowhere."

Fine, here's the key: If your answers seem to lead you nowhere, forget about getting deep insights and just get practical. Ask yourself, "What can I do to respond to what I've just read? What can I do that will express in action my desire to believe it, to take it seriously?"

When you answer this question by making a decision and doing what you decide, you will have prayed with Scripture and prayed successfully.

The words of God are not meant merely to enlighten us; they are meant to cast light on a path. Jesus called himself not just the truth, but "the way and the truth and the life." His truth shows us the way that leads to life. His school is not a school of academic learning; it is a vocational school, a school for "hands-on" learning. The Bible is a handbook for action. If we do not read God's words as invitations calling for a response, we will never understand them. If we do not read God's words with the intention of making choices in response, then none of our thoughts will lead us anywhere, because we will be asking for directions without intending to go anywhere. When we do that, we lose contact with Jesus. Jesus speaks to those who want to follow.

Saint Teresa of Avila, after explaining to her contemplative nuns seven levels of intimacy with God, ranging from bare acquaintance to "spiritual mar-

riage," and describing various levels of prayer—
prayers of petition, meditation, contemplation, the
prayer of quiet, the prayer of union, visions, locutions
and raptures—says at the end of *The Interior Castle*,
"This is the reason for prayer, my daughters, and the
purpose of this spiritual marriage: the birth always of
good works, good works."[1]

Teresa says, "The important thing is not to think
much, but to love much," and so in prayer we should
do whatever best stirs us to love. And love, she repeats
over and over, "does not consist in great delight but in
desiring with strong determination to please God in
everything...."[2] Love is shown in action.

When we pray with Scripture deep feelings and
great thoughts matter far less than whether or not we
find something to which we can respond through our
choices and actions. If we find that, we have prayed
well.

This is not the only way to pray with Scripture; it
is simply the prayer of discipleship. It is an entry-level
method for meditating on the word of God. It is down-
to-earth and practical. Its focus is on learning new attitudes and values from Jesus Christ, understanding his
reasons for them and responding to him in practical,
concrete decisions.

That is why our decisions must be something we
are actually able to do. In this kind of prayer it is perfectly acceptable, even desirable, to let our hearts
stretch out in desires without limit, longing for the
total perfection and union that as yet are still beyond
our reach. It is good to beg God to change us. But to

make sure our feet are on the ground and actually moving over it, we end our prayer with some concrete decision to do something we actually have the power to do right here and now.

If we don't feel capable of doing what we think we should do, then we should do something we *can* do. We need to take a first step, choose some means that will help us arrive at our end, concentrate on forward motion. If we can't immediately break the habit of using bad language, for example, we can fine ourselves every time we curse. It is better to pledge a rock and deliver than to promise the moon and just dream about it. When Jesus urged us to sell everything we have in order to buy the "treasure hidden in a field," he didn't exclude the installment plan. Even the "pearl of great price" can be put on layaway.

To pray with Scripture, then, just means to read a passage from the Bible and think about it until you come to a decision about something you are actually able to do.

The key words are *until* and *able*.

The Choice to Be a Disciple

Anyone can be a disciple of Jesus Christ. Everyone is invited. We just have to choose it. The choice really comes down to one thing: giving it some time. If we choose to invest some time in learning from Jesus Christ, we are choosing to be disciples. If we don't choose to invest the time, we are choosing not to be disciples. It is as simple as that.

While the amount of time you invest does have something to do with becoming a disciple, the reality of discipleship is measured not by hours, but by seriousness. Learning from Jesus is less a matter of fixed time than of constant preoccupation. Disciples of Jesus Christ always, in one way or another, reflect on his words, practice the responses he calls for, cultivate the attitudes he teaches, live out the values he exemplifies and strive for the goals he proposes.

We are not fully, authentically disciples of Jesus Christ until our life is characterized by reflection on his words and example. A disciple is someone who is always learning, and always applying what has been learned in order to learn more. A disciple automatically, spontaneously, even unconsciously, thinks with the thoughts and images of Jesus, speaks with the vocabulary of Jesus, sees everything through the eyes of Jesus, judges everything by the light of his teachings and compares everything to his example.

The disciples of Jesus are so filled with the words and images of Scripture that in everything they do and say their Christianity is evident to the people around them. Their friends catch on after a while to the fact that, no matter what situation arises, disciples are going to react from a background of principles drawn from the example and words of Jesus. More often than not, they do this without explicitly mentioning Jesus at all. They reflect him more than they refer to him.

For discipleship to permeate and characterize one's life in this way, formal, fixed periods of study are necessary. This need not be academic study, but it will surely be time given to reading, to listening to tapes or speakers, to reflection, to meditation and prayer, to liturgy, to self-evaluation, to "progress reports" and coaching through the Sacrament of Reconciliation or in spiritual direction. Some people have more time to devote to this than others, and at some periods in our life we need to give more time to it. But one thing is certain: To be disciples we have to spend enough time to be able to say with credibility that we are seriously studying the words and example of Jesus Christ, that we are real students of his. If we don't have time to give to this, we need to take a long, hard look at our priorities.

Checking the Foundation

If we can't find time to be disciples, we need to go back and look again at the "act of life-giving despair" that was the foundation of our decision to be Christian. Is Jesus an extra in our life? Can we get along without him? Can we get along without really knowing what he teaches—in depth and in breadth? Do the Ten Commandments tell us everything we need to know? If they do, what do we believe about Jesus as teacher?

If we don't spend time learning from Jesus, on what level will we interact with him? How productive will our relationship with him be? How can he, as light of the world, save us from the infecting darkness of the culture in our family and social life, in our business and politics, if we don't give time to learning from him? If we don't listen to what he says, contemplate what he does, reflect on what he teaches, how can he save our lives from destructiveness and distortion, from mediocrity and meaninglessness? Is it going to be by magic?

The Second Grave: Dying to Lights That Blind Us

To be a disciple, then, we have to enter a second grave and rise from it. We have to die to whatever keeps us from giving time and attention to learning from Jesus Christ. That might be work, it might be entertainment, it might be an all-absorbing dedication to some other field of study, it might just be laziness or inertia. Whatever it is, we have to die to our obsession with it if we want to live.

Ultimately, we have to die to the trust we place in the lights and guidance of this world. We have to die to any assumption that by living as everyone else lives, adopting the goals everyone else adopts and the attitudes everyone else accepts, following the priorities everyone else follows, we can find fulfillment and happiness. We have to get serious about learning a new way to live.

This is what frees us to be disciples. And the first thing we have to look at is the use we make of time.

In the Ten Commandments God prescribed a weekly day of leisure, the Sabbath. This commandment was a pedagogical device; its purpose was to teach God's people something. According to the rabbis, the purpose of the Sabbath is to teach us that human beings are different from the rest of creation. Everything else in the universe gets its reason for existence from what it contributes to the functioning of the planet. For that reason, nothing in nature "rests" unless there is a reason for resting or unless there is no reason to work. The sun comes up every day, the grass grows and animals hunt for food until they are tired or satisfied.

But humans are told to rest one day a week, whether there is work to be done or not, whether they are tired or not, whether there is any reason for resting or not and whether they like it or not. The purpose of the day of leisure is to say to us that we humans do not derive our whole reason for existing from what we contribute to the planet by our work. Work is an important element of human life, but it is not life's whole purpose. We have a direct, immediate relationship with God. We were made for God. We exist for God. Our lives have absolute value from that fact alone, whether they seem to contribute anything to the well-being of the planet or not.

To get that point across, God told his people that on one day a week they should do no work—that is, do nothing that they would do just because it has to get done (barring emergencies, of course). That is what work is: something we do that is not just for fun. Through the Sabbath observance they were to express and experience the fact that human beings exist not just to get things done, but for relationship with God.

When we are so absorbed by our work and our duties that we have no time for discipleship, no time to cultivate knowledge and love of God through relationship with Jesus Christ, no time to learn from the word of God, then we lose what the Sabbath law was established to give, regardless of what we do or don't do on Sundays. When we have no leisure time to spend on God (and a quick trip to Sunday Mass is not leisure time), we are missing the lesson of the Sabbath observance, and we are not keeping the commandment, "Remember to keep holy the Sabbath day."

Some people are not free to keep the Sabbath. Slaves, for example, are not free. And many people today feel they are slaves of an economic system that requires them to work without respite. Many businesses stay open on Sunday. Many people work two jobs. Many people with only one job have other responsibilities, such as family, which seem to take up every minute of their time, every day of the week. Those who are caught in these situations must judge for themselves whether they are truly free. If they are not free they are not guilty of breaking the law of the Sabbath. But guilty or not, unless they do something to compensate they will suffer the loss of what the Sabbath observance was designed to give, and that is a serious loss.

When we really are free to take the leisure called for by the Sabbath observance but our own priorities prevent us from keeping this commandment, we have to ask ourselves seriously whether something has gone awry in our guidance system. We might be living for the wrong goals in life. We might be expending all our energy only to find that we're heading in the wrong direction.

To take the second step into the fullness of life, then, we have to die to our presumption that what most people *think* is important really *is* important. We have to die to the idea that success as defined in our culture is important, or that the prestige and status we can win in this world through wealth and success have any value at all. We have to take a lot of false goals (which are really false gods) down into the grave with us and rise up from the grave without them. We have to die to the things that take up our time and give energy to cultivating relationship with the One who gave us time precisely for this purpose: that we might cultivate relationship with himself.

For us "time" and "life" are coterminous. Time begins for us when our life begins, and when our life ends that is the end of our time. What we spend our time on is what we spend our life on. When our time is gone, our life on this earth is over, spent. What kind of life we have after that depends on what we have spent our time on, how we have invested it.

This is not just a long-term investment. What we spend our time on now determines what kind of life we have right now. God gives us our time for whatever purpose he gives us our life. They are one and the same gift. Therefore, if we say we "don't have any time" to spend on learning to know and love God, we are saying that we have not received life for that purpose—a serious mistake.

The reality is, we were created to know God, to love God and to serve God on this earth and be united with him in perfect joy forever. This is all we have time for, because it is all we have life for. Without giving time to discipleship we won't know enough about God to love him as we should, and we won't know how to serve him as he desires. That is a good reason to become a disciple.

If we want to enter into life, then, the second step is to make the choice to lead a life characterized by reflection on the message of Jesus. This is the choice to be a disciple.

Questions for Reflection and Discussion

- *What would it mean for me, in my circumstances, to live a life "characterized by reflection on the message of Jesus"? What would it look like? How would it show?*

- *What really keeps me from reading Scripture every day? What is the answer to this dilemma?*

- *What area in my life could benefit from my learning more about the attitudes, values and promises of Jesus?*

- *What concrete and specific actions can I take to be a disciple of Jesus Christ? How, when, where will I begin?*

Notes

[1] *The Interior Castle*, "The Seventh Dwelling Places," no. 6, in *The Collected Works of St. Teresa of Avila*, translated by Kavanaugh and Rodriguez (Washington, D.C.: ICS Publications 1980), p. 446.
[2] Ibid., "The Fourth Dwelling Places," no. 7, p. 319.

■

The Choice to Be a Prophet

*Dying to Social Conformity;
Rising to Prophetic Witness*

The third step is the choice to make everything in my life and life-style bear witness to Jesus Christ. This is what it means to accept my baptismal commitment as prophet. To do this I have to die to fear of standing alone through personal decisions. This is the third grave.

A Christian prophet is not someone who foretells the future, but someone who creates it. Prophets lead the Church into the future by embodying the future in their own lives. The actions of the prophets are embodied previews of a new level of morality, a new expression of grace, a new response to the needs of our times.

The problem with being a prophet is that no one likes to stand alone, not even before the silent tribunal of one's own heart. We don't like to take the responsibility of making deep moral decisions all by ourselves. We prefer to expand conscience to a committee.

The easiest, most common way to do this is just to follow the crowd. This is called cultural or social conformity. A second, more religious way is to abdicate personal judgment in favor of law-observance. This is called legalism. If we want to be prophets we have to break free of cultural conformity and go beyond law observance. In both cases we are giving up the sense of security that is found in the middle of a crowd. We are accepting the challenge to stand alone. We were consecrated at Baptism to do this.

What Is a Prophet?

In general, a prophet is anyone who professes the truth of God publicly. We exercise our baptismal consecration as prophets every time we make the sign of the cross in public, enter a church or genuflect to the tabernacle. We are living up to our commitment as prophets when we speak up in defense of the truth or live out the teachings of Jesus. Any act of Christian witness is an act of prophecy, of professing faith in Jesus Christ. To be a witness and to be a prophet are one and the same thing.

In a more particular way, however, a Christian prophet is someone who takes the general, abstract principles of the gospel and applies them creatively to the concrete circumstances of a given time and place.

Jesus seldom, if ever, made rules; rather, he taught principles. Aristotle defines a principle as "that from which something begins." A moral principle is a statement from which moral reflection begins. For example, when Jesus says, "Love one another as I love you" (John 15:12d) that is a principle. We can't just go out and do it; we have to think about what it means in practice. We have to make judgments: Who is my neighbor? What does it mean to love this particular neighbor, here and now, as Jesus has loved me?

A principle requires us to think, to decide for ourselves what these words call us to do in the concrete, practical reality of our own lives. The principle gives us a starting point, but before we can act we have to reach our own conclusion.

A law, on the other hand, can make us think we have no more judgments to make. A law tells us exactly what to do. We might say that moral reflection begins with principles and ends (for a community, at least) with laws. The space in between is for prophets.[1]

Prophetic witness is frequently a preview of law. For example, "Love one another as I love you" was not specific enough to tell Christians that racial segregation was a sin. For eighteen hundred years it didn't even tell them that slavery was a sin. And so, when the prophets stood up in Alabama and Mississippi in the fifties and took a stand on the gospel against segregation, they stood on principle in the absence of adequate laws. But because of their witness the Church recognized that segregation was a failure to apply the teaching of Jesus to the concrete reality of the situation in the South. And so the Church officially abolished segregation in the churches—and converted prophecy into law.

But between the principle and the law stood the prophets. If they had not gone beyond the laws in their thinking—and expressed this in their action—Jesus' principle of loving as he loves would never have been applied to the racial situation in the United States. It would not have taken flesh in action or in law.

Before the principles of the gospel can be embodied in laws, they have to be embodied in Christian witness. Prophets create the future.

The Unwritten Laws of Practice

The word *law* can mean more than explicit rules and regulations. Unwritten laws govern much of what is done within a culture.

The most dangerous laws are the unwritten ones that proclaim by their absence that something is permissible when it is not. There was an unwritten law—common Christian practice—that said slavery was permissible when it was not. Another unwritten law—the silent Christian acceptance of segregation—said that racial discrimination was permissible when it was not. What the Church does not say has as much influence on our lives as what it does say.

The voice that will break this silence—the only voice that can break it—is the voice of the prophets. The official voices in the Church, the pastors, the bishops, the hierarchy, are the voices of stabilizing authority, not of groundbreaking prophecy. Church officials are commissioned and charged to be public voices, not private ones. They speak for what is already accepted, already authorized or already seen clearly enough to be authorized and legislated in the community. It is unfair to expect the voice of public authority to be the voice of private inspiration.

And yet, official voices frequently are prophetic. When bishops and pastors speak, not just as official teachers of approved doctrine and law but also as ordained preachers of the gospel, they frequently speak as prophets. Then they receive from the Church as well as from the world a "prophet's reward"—resistance and rejection packaged with persecution. At such times, more often than not, those Christians who have been the most vocal about the need for obedience and law-observance in the Church close ranks and turn violently against the authority they idolized.

How to Become a Prophet

Theologically, no Christian has to become a prophet; we were all made prophets—consecrated and empowered to be prophets—when we were anointed with chrism at Baptism.

But what we are and what we actually do are frequently out of step with each other. We do not become fully what we are until our doing matches our being. We do not enter into the reality of our baptismal consecration as prophets until we consciously recognize and accept on a personal level our commitment to bear prophetic witness.

What does this mean in concrete terms? When are we really—personally and practically—committed to being prophets? It is well and good to say, "I commit myself to receiving prophetic insights!" but that does not mean we will receive them. We can also commit ourselves to the work of a prophet, which is to apply creatively the general, abstract teachings of Jesus to the concrete circumstances of our own time and place. But will we know how to apply them? Will we see how they apply?

In spelling out the prophetic commitment, we take for granted that one has already taken the first two steps into the fullness of Christian life, that is, that one is already committed to being both a Christian and a disciple.

A prophet acts as the Body of Christ, the Word of God made flesh. In the prophet the words of Jesus are made flesh in action. This means that to be prophets we must be committed to making Jesus Christ a part of everything we do. And to be prophets we must be disciples. We cannot hope to see how the words of Jesus apply to life in our time and place unless we are familiar with those words. We can't apply the gospel to life unless we are studying the gospel. But granted the first two commitments, the commitment to being a prophet breaks down into two other concrete choices, which are really one and the same.

Changing the Moral Question

We enter into the life of prophetic witness on the day we change our standard of morality. The prophet is one who makes the choice never to ask again merely whether something is right or wrong, but whether it bears witness to Jesus Christ.

John Paul II wrote in *The Splendor of Truth*, "Following Christ is thus the essential and primordial foundation of Christian morality.... Jesus' way of acting and his words, his deeds and his precepts constitute the moral rule of Christian life." And in his World Day of Peace address for January 1, 1993, he said, "Christ's example, no less than his words, is normative for Christians."[2] Taken seriously, these words will revolutionize moral theology. The prophet takes them seriously.

The prophet doesn't ask, "Is it wrong to speak like this, to dress like this, to spend money like this, to spend time on this?" The prophet asks, "Does it bear witness to the values taught by Jesus Christ if I speak like this, dress like this, spend time or money on this?"

A law-observer asks, "Is it wrong to leave this person out of a party?" A prophet answers, "That is the wrong question. The real question is, does it bear witness to Jesus Christ if you leave that person out of the party?"

A law-observer asks, "Is it wrong for me to go

along with this policy where I work?" A prophet answers, "It is not enough to approach it that way. Ask instead, does it bear witness to Jesus Christ if you go along with that policy?"

Don't Oversimplify

These are not simple questions. We do not always bear authentic witness to Jesus Christ by doing the most idealistic thing—even though more commonly we fail to bear witness when we do nothing. Jesus said we are to be "shrewd as serpents and simple as doves" (Matthew 10:16). Simple does not mean simplistic. There are usually many factors to take into consideration when we make a concrete moral decision. The prophet has to weigh them all. It is not an easy task.

When a decision is simple enough to be easy, there is usually a law to cover it. We are talking here about the territory beyond the law, where the path is not marked and we have only a general direction to follow. Law-observers steer by the channel markers of the Ten Commandments; their course is to keep within bounds. Prophets steer by the fixed star that is Jesus Christ; their course is to direct their lives toward him. They have to navigate.

The commitment to be a prophet is not a commitment to find the right answers; it is a commitment to ask the right questions.

The prophet learns by trial and error how to discern the truth. Often we are afraid to be prophets because we are afraid to make mistakes. We are afraid to make personal decisions when we have no way of knowing whether we are right or not, even after we have made them. Thus the prophet has to die to fear, beginning with the fear of being wrong.

A Commitment to Continual Conversion

The second commitment involved in the choice to be a prophet is the commitment to continual conversion.

Since *conversion* has become a religious word, we can expect it to have lost its meaning. If we pledge ourselves right now to "continual conversion of life," to what are we committing ourselves? What are we actually going to do? If, a year from now, each of us asked, "Am I more converted to Jesus than I was last year?" would we know the answer?

"I don't know." "Maybe." "I suppose so." "I hope so."

So let's change the word. Let's use a real word instead. Suppose we all commit ourselves today to "continual change." Suppose each one of us stands before Jesus Christ and says, "Lord, I promise you that I will make continual changes in my life-style. I don't know how many; I don't know how often. But I will start making changes and I will continue." If we ask ourselves a year later what changes we have made, every one of us will know exactly what to say. Either there will be concrete changes we can point to or there won't be.

This is the commitment that makes us prophets. The commitment to continuing conversion, to constant change of life-style and behavior, is a commitment that says *what* we will do. The commitment to bear witness says *how* we will do it. If we commit ourselves to keep changing, we will evaluate everything in our life and life-style in light of the way it bears witness to the teaching and example of Jesus Christ.

The commitment to keep changing gets us moving; the commitment to bear witness gives us direction. Together (and presupposing discipleship) they guarantee that we will discover new and creative ways to apply the gospel to life, that we will receive prophetic insights.

To become a prophet, then, we must begin looking systematically into every element and expression of our life-style, asking about each one: "How does this—or how could this—bear witness to the teaching of Jesus Christ?" We must look at how we spend our time, how we spend our money, what we eat and drink, how we speak to people at home and at work, how we dress and drive. We must look at the policies we establish or follow in our profession, at the goals we pursue and the means we take to achieve them. We must begin reshaping, reordering our lives according to the pattern taught and modeled by Jesus in the Gospels.

Is this a commitment you are willing to make? If not, then change the question. Ask, "Is this a commitment I will to make?" If you will it, you are willing. If you do not will it—if you do not choose to do it—Jesus offers three reasons that might tell you why.[3]

The Beaten Path. Jesus said (Matthew 13) that the first reason the seed of his word does not grow in our hearts is that it falls on the "beaten path" of social conformity. When gospel teachings contradict what everyone is doing, those teachings may not even register with us. We tend to take it for granted that what "everyone" (especially if they are churchgoing Christians) is doing must be what Jesus teaches. We interpret what Christ says by what Christians do instead of measuring what Christians do by what Christ says.

Jesus said, "By their fruits you will know them" (Matthew 7:16). If, however, we begin with the mistaken assumption that the most common fruit on the market must be good fruit, we have no standard by which to judge. By uncritically swallowing the fruit of mediocre Christianity, we lose our taste for the root, for the radical call of the gospel. We rule out any radical summons of Christ that here and now is falling on the ears of Christians who refuse to hear.

We have to take a pickax to the "beaten path" of social conformity. We have to despair of reaching fulfillment by letting our lives take their course, by letting them follow the course society, even our so-called Christian society, lays down for them. We have to decide instead to give Jesus Christ as Savior an active role in every area of our lives. This is a radical break with culture, and it is the real decision to be a *Christian*.

The Rocky Ground. The second reason the seed does not grow is that it falls on rocky ground that has no depth. The roots never take hold. This is what happens when we do not reflect on the words of Jesus long enough to come to some decisions; when we do not think about his teaching until our thinking leads us to choices; in other words, when our response stops short.

Nothing is really a part of us until we have made it our own by making choices. No truth is rooted in our soul until we respond to it in free decisions. To commit ourselves to a life of thinking and responding to the gospel is to become a *disciple*. This is what gives our soul depth for the seed of God to grow.

Seed Among Thorns. But Jesus pointed out a third obstacle to the growth of his word in our hearts: In untended ground weeds and brambles choke out the plant as soon as it begins to sprout. To let the word of God grow to fruition in us, we need to weed the garden. We need to get rid of whatever is in conflict with the ideals, the goals, the attitudes and values of Jesus, because these obstacles block our sight.

Weeding means deliberately attacking those desires and fears that may be blinding us—including those we think are not in our way at all. We never know how dirty our glasses are until we clean them off. The fastest way to do this is to make a commitment to continual change. First we promise God changes; then we start making them; in the process we discover what in our life needs to be changed. We commit to the *what* that will open our eyes to the *how*.

We start making changes in an effort to make

every visible element of our life-style express the attitudes and values of Jesus. Then we begin to see.

This means action. It means physical, concrete choices. It means getting practical about applying the gospel to real life. It means making our lives fit the gospel instead of adapting the gospel to fit our lives.

This is religion in flesh and blood, religion that can be seen, heard, tasted and felt. This is what it means to be a prophet.

A car's headlights illumine the road for three hundred feet ahead. If we never move the car we will never see farther than three hundred feet. Life is the same: If we want to see we have to move. If we want to receive prophetic insights we have to get ourselves in gear.

If we read the gospel and admire it, but do not act on what we see, we will never see anything more. But if we commit ourselves to changes, to advancing even when the light is blocked, we will discover what obstacles obscure our vision. If we commit to forward motion so that we have to remove the obstacles in order to keep it going, then we will begin to see more and more and more.

Once we are doing what we can as disciples to learn the truth of Jesus, the obstacle to prophetic insight will be in the heart, not in the head. Clarity of mind is obscured by attachments of the heart. But if we purify our hearts by making our behavior conform to what we see in the gospel, we will "see and understand." Jesus promised, "Blessed are the clean of heart, for they will see God" (Matthew 5:8).

This is the key to prophetic witness.

The Third Grave: Dying to Fear and Desire

To live up to our baptismal consecration as prophets, then, we have to die to our desire for anything that stands as an obstacle to the growth of God's seed in our hearts. We have to die to everything that keeps us from living God's life to the full. We have to do this whether others seem concerned about it or not. We have to be willing to stand alone.

To do this we have to enter into a third grave. We have to die to our fear of standing alone. We have to die to our fear of making personal, risky decisions. We have to die to social conformity and to our need for approval and crowd support.

The way we die to fears and desires is simply to act against them. The emotions don't go away. We can't remain paralyzed until we stop feeling afraid of what we know cannot harm us, or until we stop feeling desire for what we know cannot satisfy us. If we wait until we stop feeling fear and desire we will wait until we are dead. But if we choose to die to our fears and desires by acting as if they did not exist, we will free ourselves to live.

The way to do this is simple: just do it. We stand before Jesus Christ and promise that we will begin making changes in our life. And we promise that we will make them not by asking what is right and wrong, but by asking how every choice and element of our life-style can bear witness to the truth Jesus teaches, to the values he proclaims.

We can even be systematic about it if we choose. We can begin going through our room, our house, our worksite, looking at what is there and asking how it bears witness to the message of Jesus Christ, what it says about our response to his Good News. We can look at how we spend our money, our time; how we choose our friends, our books, our cars, our clothes, our food and drink. If we do this with freedom, making it more like a hobby than a task, it can be enjoyable, even intriguing. We may learn a lot about the all-embracing scope of God's appreciation for the world. We may discover how things with no immediately evident religious value testify in fact to God's love for the world and for us who use and enjoy his creation.

We may also find ourselves invited to a generosity beyond our wildest imaginings—and responding to the invitation with great joy. We may experience ourselves living "life to the full." The key is to do this not as an obligation that arouses guilt, but as a voluntary project that aims at a richer, fuller response to Jesus Christ.

We don't have to be heroic. We don't have to do it all at once. We just have to begin. To do this is to live up to our baptismal consecration as prophets.

Questions for Reflection and Discussion

■ *What is there in my life-style—that is, in the way I live, work, play and take part in shaping society—that shows I believe in Jesus Christ?*

■ *What experience have I had of going beyond laws—or seeing others go beyond laws—to apply the principles of Jesus to concrete situations here and now?*

■ *What difference would it make in my life if I decided to ask in every decision that I make, "How will this bear witness to my belief in Jesus Christ?"*

■ *What concrete and specific actions can I take to begin systematically to make everything in my life and life-style bear witness to the teachings and values of Jesus? How, when, where will I start?*

Notes

[1] To do merely what the law says is standard practice, but it is not really the Christian way of observing laws. Nothing ever exempts a Christian from thinking. Christians are required to make a personal judgment in each case, applying the law to the reality they are dealing with and asking whether in this particular situation a literal observance of the law will bring about the result the lawgiver intended and desires.

[2] *The Splendor of Truth*, #19-20; *Origins* 22/28, Dec. 29, 1992.

[3] These are taken from the parable of the sower, Matthew 13:1-23. They are developed in my book *His Word* (St. Anthony Messenger Press, 1986; reprinted by His Way Communications, 1995).

STEP FOUR

———————————■———————————

The Choice to Be a Priest

Dying to Self-enclosed Religion;
Rising to Ministry

The fourth step is the choice to mediate the life of God to others. This is what it means to accept my baptismal commitment as priest. To do this I have to die to fear of revealing myself through self-expression. This is the fourth grave.

Many of us grew up thinking that religion was the way to get to heaven. We saw religion as the way to live a good life, to be a good person, to become personally pleasing to God.

Ministry was for those called to be ministers: priests, nuns, deacons, lay missionaries, lay professionals in church work and those laypersons who could devote themselves to part-time activities in the parish: eucharistic ministers, visitors to the sick, members of the pastoral council.

We may never have thought of ourselves as being consecrated and committed to full-time ministry in the Church simply by the fact of Baptism. If so, perhaps we never really thought about the words spoken to us at Baptism when we were anointed with chrism: "God the Father of our Lord Jesus Christ has freed you from sin, given you a new birth by water and the Holy Spirit, and welcomed you into his holy people. He now anoints you with the chrism of salvation. As Christ was anointed Priest, Prophet, and King, so may you live always as a member of his body, sharing everlasting life."

We were anointed priests by God. *Chrism* is the word from which "Christ"—"the Anointed"—was taken. By Baptism we became members of Christ the Anointed One. As members of Christ we share in his anointing as Prophet, Priest and King. By this anointing we are consecrated, empowered and committed to carry on the mission of Jesus as prophets, priests and stewards of his kingship. This is the "job description" of a Christian.

We have seen what it means to be a prophet. Now we need to look at what it means to be a priest, what it means to share by Baptism in the priesthood of Jesus. To accept this priesthood, to which we were already consecrated in Baptism, is the fourth step into the fullness of life.

Dying to Self-centeredness; Rising to Community

Priesthood is only intelligible within a context and acceptance of community. Those who receive the sacrament of Holy Orders are never ordained for their private, personal benefit. They are ordained to serve the community, and only to serve the community. Ordination to priesthood is ordination to service, to ministry, to the washing of feet and to availability in love.

This is true of all priesthood. Such was Jesus' priesthood, which is the only priesthood that remains. Jesus "did not come to be served but to serve and to give his life as a ransom for many" (Matthew 20:28). This is what priesthood is, then: serving and dying, giving oneself for the life of the world. All who are baptized into Christ are baptized into this priesthood, into Christ's priesthood. To be baptized is to be consecrated to ministry, to service, to dying to one's self in order to live totally for God and for other people in love. It is to accept the community dimension of our religion and give ourselves as bread to be broken and eaten for the life of the world. What Jesus said to Peter he says to us: "Do you love me? ...Feed my sheep" (John 21:17).

To take on our baptismal commitment as priests, then, we have to die to any notion we might have that religion is a private affair. To be authentic Christians we have to accept our relationship to God as relationship within a community. We have to die to the idea that we can stand before God as private individuals without any responsibility for the rest of the community, for the rest of the human race.

Religion hasn't been a private affair since the Lord first said to Cain, "Where is your brother Abel?" and Cain made the mistake of answering, "I do not know; am I my brother's keeper?"

For Jews and Christians religion has not been a private affair since God first made a covenant with Israel; since Jesus first entrusted his message to a community and, together with the Father, poured out the Holy Spirit on an assembly instead of on a single individual.[1]

Religion has not been a private affair for any one of us since the day we were anointed at Baptism to be priests. Priesthood is ministry within a community, and on the day of our Baptism we were consecrated as priests to minister within the community of the Church.

Mediating the Life of God

To minister as priests is *to mediate the life of God to others in love*. This sounds exalted. But what does it mean on ground level?

What did God do when he came to be our priest? He took flesh. Jesus is the Word made flesh. He is the embodied expression of the truth, the love of God. As such, he gave life to the world.

If we accept the priesthood to which we are consecrated and committed by Baptism, we undertake to do exactly the same thing: to let the grace that is within us take flesh in physical expression. We dedicate ourselves to being the embodied expression of the divine truth and love of God—for the life of the world.

In short, we dedicate ourselves to *expressing* our faith, to expressing our hope, to expressing our love in ways that give life to the community of faith and to every individual we meet. When we give physical expression in words and gestures to the invisible truth that is in our minds by faith, then we are using our humanity to mediate truth to others. When the invisible word of faith in our minds becomes a spoken word of witness on our lips, then our bodies become the medium through which the divine truth of God is communicated to others.

The spiritual words God speaks in our hearts take flesh when we speak them with our lips. To do this is to let our humanity, our physical bodies mediate the truth of God to others. To become the medium through which Jesus' words of truth are given to others is to become the medium through which his life is given to others. It is to mediate life in love. This is priesthood. The same is true of all the ways in which we embody God's love to others. When we express our love sexually to a spouse or express it in physical, non-sexual ways to others; when we care for the sick, give help to the poor, show compassion for those who are afflicted or simply smile at the people whom we serve at work, or who serve us—in all of this we mediate the love of

God to others by letting his love take flesh in our actions. This is priesthood.

Self-expression is the key to priesthood, provided we are aware that the self we are expressing is the self united to Jesus Christ, the graced self, the divine self we are because we are one with Jesus Christ, members of his body and temples of his Spirit. To be a priest is to dedicate our humanity to being the self-expression of God.

The Fourth Grave: Dying to Fear of Self-expression

Why don't we express what is inside of us? Why don't we say something to people when we see they are depressed? Why don't we break the ice and smile or say a personal word to someone? Why don't we compliment people every time we see something good in them?

Why do we kneel alone at the back of the Church during liturgy, as if we were not part of the ministering team? Why do we pick a spot as far from others as we can get, rather than pray shoulder-to-shoulder as a community? There is a time to pray alone. For that Jesus told us to go into our rooms and shut the door and pray to our Father in private. But if we try to make the Mass that kind of prayer we do not participate authentically in the Mass, and neither are we authentically alone. We falsify both kinds of prayer.

Why are we so reluctant to talk about our religion, about our prayer, about our spiritual experiences? Why are we so afraid of praying with others, even with our closest friends or family? Why are we so embarrassed about praying out loud, or about praying in our own words?

For that matter, why don't we sing in church, or at least join in the people's responses during liturgy as if we were *celebrating* Mass (as we are) instead of just absorbing it? Why don't we participate like active players who are a part of the action? Why don't we take responsibility for the overall impact the liturgy has on others as well as on ourselves?

Is it because we are there not to serve but to be served? Is it because we think the ordained priest is there to minister and we are there to be ministered to? Is it because we don't realize that the laity are priests? When we are at Mass, do we think the ordained priest can "make it happen" without us? Yes, he can make the essential action of the Mass take place whether anyone else is there are not. But even then he acts in the name of the whole Church and the whole Church speaks through him.

The ordained priest cannot make the Mass be for the congregation what it should be, and do for the congregation what it should do, unless all the members of the congregation make it their ministry to participate fully, actively and consciously so that the Mass may be and be experienced by all as what it authentically is.

Saint Paul describes the liturgy as a communal enterprise, something the whole community has a hand in creating:

> When you assemble, one has a psalm, another
> an instruction, a revelation, a tongue, or an

> interpretation.... If anyone speaks in a tongue,
> let it be two or at most three.... Two or three
> prophets should speak, and the others discern.
> But if a revelation is given to another person
> sitting there, the first one should be silent. For
> you can all prophesy one by one, so that all may
> learn and all be encouraged... (see 1 Corinthians
> 14:26-32).

This description of what people do at Mass might
sound foreign to us, but it is consistent with Paul's
teaching about the anointing we received at Baptism.
Everyone anointed to serve as prophet, priest and
steward of Christ's kingship is given gifts of ministry
through the outpouring of the Holy Spirit:

> To each individual the manifestation of the
> Spirit is given for some benefit...the expression
> of wisdom...the expression of
> knowledge...faith...gifts of healing...mighty
> deeds...prophecy...discernment of
> spirits...tongues...the interpretation of tongues.
> But one and the same Spirit produces all of
> these, distributing them individually to each
> person as he wishes (see 1 Corinthians 12:7-11).

The ways our communal participation in liturgy is
expressed can change over the ages; but the fact of that
active, creative participation in liturgy and in the life
of the Church is foundational; it is a truth upon which
liturgy is built.

The Church Saint Paul teaches us to be is a Church
in which there are many different kinds of ministries,
but everyone is a minister. Everyone receives the out-

pouring of the Holy Spirit, and everyone shares the gifts of the Spirit with others in a common ministry of "building up the body of Christ" in love. There are apostles and prophets, teachers and miracle workers, healers and helpers, administrators and leaders, speakers in tongues and interpreters of tongues (see 1 Corinthians 12:27-31). And there are many other gifts and ministries Paul doesn't list. But everyone is gifted by the Spirit and everyone is called to share that gift in ministry.

This is the law of life for those who live by the Spirit: to *share in* is to *share with*. There is no purely private, personal, individual religion in the Body of Christ. All receive life, give life and grow in life through the functioning of the whole Body and every one of its members.

The Mass is the prayer of the Church, and the Church is a community of priests. Jesus has "made us into a kingdom, priests for his God and Father" (Revelation 1:6). We are all "living stones...built into a spiritual house, to be a holy priesthood to offer spiritual sacrifices acceptable to God through Jesus Christ" (1 Peter 2:5-9).

If we are conscious of our priesthood at Mass, we will probably be conscious of it outside of Mass. What we do at Mass, what we express and experience there, has a great deal to do with the way we perceive and express ourselves as Christians at work and at home, in our social lives and in our civic activities. If we are aware at Mass that we are there to minister to others and to serve, it will be easier for us to see everything we do as priestly ministry and service. We will be more clearly aware that in everything we do, we are called to offer our flesh—and to offer grace embodied and expressed in our flesh—for the life of the world.

When we are fully conscious of being present at Mass as ministers, and of ministering at Mass as priests, then outside of Mass we will be present to everyone as ministers, and we will minister to everyone as priests. We will mediate divine life to them by letting God's light, God's love express themselves in and through our human words and actions.

It was for this that God gave us the Holy Spirit at Baptism, "to equip the saints for the work of ministry, for building up the body of Christ until all of us come to...maturity, to the full stature of Christ...from whom the whole body, as each part is working properly, promotes the body's growth in building itself up in love"](see Ephesians 4:11-16).

Dying to Fear; Rising to Ministry

A priest is someone who has accepted the ministry of mediating the life of God to others. And every Christian is consecrated to this priesthood by Baptism. So why don't we make it our constant ministry to "build up the body of Christ" in love?

Whatever the excuses we offer for not expressing our religious devotion in the sight of others, the root reason is fear. This is the fear to which we have to die: the fear of revealing ourselves to others through self-expression; the fear of nakedness. This is not always the fear of being seen as we are. It may be the fear of being seen as we are not: the fear that others will perceive us as being on the "freaky" side.

We are afraid that if we express what is deep within us, the expression won't match what we feel or won't do it justice or won't be understood or simply won't be acceptable to the people we are with. Or we may be afraid that something deep within us will be desecrated by a lack of appreciation. Even Jesus had something to say about not tossing pearls to the wrong people (Matthew 7:6).

Sometimes we are simply afraid of being identified with the kind of people whose religious emotionalism has turned us off. We have had people force their religion on us, and we don't want to appear to be doing the same thing.

If you can identify with what has just been said, there is no danger you will sin by excess in the revelation of yourself. People who are keenly aware of the cliff seldom go over the edge. Those who worry about falling into sentimentality or emotionalism never come close to it.

The Nakedness of God

If the reasons we give for not revealing ourselves to others are valid, then God should never have taken flesh in Jesus. God knew that if he revealed his true self to the human race, his attitudes and values would be misunderstood and rejected. *He* would be misunderstood and rejected.

God also knew that there was no way any human self-expression, even through the humanity of Jesus, could begin to do justice to the divine truth and beauty of his person. If we hold back from revealing our deepest, most intimate selves because we fear the desecration of nonappreciation, what must God have felt at the prospect of letting the inmost truth of his being, the Word, the second Person of the Trinity, appear in the limitations of human flesh before the eyes of the human race?

Is is too much to ask, as Saint Paul does, that we should let the same mind, the same attitude, be in us "that was in Christ Jesus"

> who, though he was in the form of God,
> did not regard equality with God something to
>   be exploited,
> but emptied himself, taking the form of a slave,
> being born in human likeness.
> And being found in human form, he humbled
>   himself.... (see Philippians 2:5-8)

If God was not afraid to take the risk of revealing himself in Jesus Christ, the Word of God made flesh, should we be afraid of revealing ourselves by giving human expression to the words God speaks in our hearts?

The fourth step, then, is the commitment to mediate the life of God to others by letting the light and love of God that are within us express themselves in and through our human actions. To do this we have to die to our fear of self-expression. We have to die to any desire we might have to keep our religion a private affair between ourselves and God. We have to commit ourselves to the ministry of self-revelation, which was the ministry of the Word made flesh.

If we enter into this fourth grave, we can rise free to share with others the light and love of God that are within us. We can let our human flesh be what it was consecrated at Baptism to be: the Body of Christ mediating the life of God to others, his flesh given for the life of the world. This is priesthood. It is dying to self in order to live totally for God and other people in love. It takes the form of self-expression. And we are called to it. If we are obedient to that call it can lead us "to the point of death—even death on a cross."

Questions for Reflection and Discussion

- *Why do I need to minister to others in order to be authentically Christian? Does this mean I have to take an active part in what the Christian community does?*

- *Specifically, why do I need to express my faith, my hope, my love to others in order to be Christian? Why can't I just keep my religion between myself and God?*

- *Why am I so afraid to express my thoughts, my feelings about God? For example, do I feel reluctant to pray out loud with others? To do so in my own words? To share with others my thoughts about a passage in the*

Scriptures? To talk about my experience of God?

■ *What can I do to live up to my baptismal consecration as priest? How can I mediate the life of God to others by giving physical expression to the divine truth, the divine love, that are within me? Concretely and specifically, how, when, where will I do this?*

Notes

[1] The word *church*—in Greek *ekklesia*—means "assembly."

STEP FIVE

———————◼———————

The Choice to Be a Steward

*Dying to Noninvolvement;
Rising to Responsibility for the Kingdom*

The fifth step is the choice to take responsibility for transforming the world as a steward of Christ's kingship. This is what it means to accept my baptismal consecration as king. To do this I have to die to any sense of hopelessness or discouragement about the effect I can have on the world. This is the fifth grave.

Jesus' first recorded preaching was, "The kingdom of God has come near." His last recorded act was to turn over to us the responsibility for establishing it.

Jesus began his public career by proclaiming, "This is the time of fulfillment. The kingdom of God is at hand. Repent, and believe in the gospel" (Mark 1:15).

In his native town of Nazareth, when Jesus stood up to read in the synagogue, the text he chose was:

> "The Spirit of the Lord is upon me,
> because he has anointed me
> to bring glad tidings to the poor.
> He has sent me to proclaim liberty to captives
> and recovery of sight to the blind,
> to let the oppressed go free."
>   Rolling up the scroll, he handed it back to
> the attendant and sat down, and the eyes of all
> in the synagogue looked intently at him. He
> said to them, "Today this scripture passage is
> fulfilled in your hearing" (Luke 4:18-21).

And it is still being fulfilled. To understand Jesus, we have to understand him as a working Messiah. And we have to work with him. The last thing he did before he ascended into heaven was to turn over his mission to us:

> "All power in heaven and on earth has been
> given to me. Go, therefore, and make disciples
> of all nations, baptizing them in the name of the
> Father, and of the Son, and of the Holy Spirit,
> teaching them to observe all that I have
> commanded you. And behold, I am with you
> always, until the end of the age" (Matthew
> 28:18-20).

The fifth step into the fullness of life is to take responsibility for carrying out this command.

Religion Without Religiosity

To "make disciples of all nations...teaching them to observe all that I have commanded you" does not mean simply teaching the catechism to people all over the world. It means penetrating every area of human life and activity with the principles, values, attitudes and priorities Jesus modeled and taught.

It means transforming everything people do on this earth—in family and social life, in business and politics—by bringing them under the life-giving reign of Christ.

This is not to impose some kind of restrictive religious rule on all the activities that are natural to life in this world. It doesn't mean to falsify the nature of business and politics, of education and family life, by directing these to some artificial "religious" end instead of to their natural goal and purpose. Above all, it doesn't mean putting the Church in charge of things the Church was never meant to be in charge of.

What it does mean is for Christians to bring the light and love of Christ into everything people do on earth so that every activity people engage in might be more authentically, more fully what it was intended to be in the first place—and more.

Grace can lift up every human activity to a higher level, to the level of God's own activity and fruitfulness. Grace means sharing in God's divine life through union with Jesus Christ. It makes us and everything we do divine. Those who accept that they are the Body of Christ by grace hear spoken to them an echo of the words Elizabeth spoke to Mary: "Blessed is the fruit of your *life*." What we do in union with Jesus Christ will have value that endures forever.

But grace never destroys nature. Jesus said of the law God gave to the Chosen People through Moses: "Do not think that I have come to abolish the law or the prophets. I have come not to abolish but to fulfill" (Matthew 5:17). He also says this about every human action and enterprise transformed by grace. Christians acting in union with God by grace respect the integrity of everything they deal with; they leave nature intact. God the Redeemer does not act in contradiction to God the Creator.

To transform and renew society by grace, the first thing Christians have to do is recognize and respect the true, natural purpose of what they are trying to transform. Business needs to be transformed into better business, not into "works of charity." Education needs to be transformed into better education, not into glorified Bible study. Politics needs to be transformed into better politics, not into the servant of ecclesiastical policies. And social life, to be Christian, needs to look more like the wedding feast of Cana than a picnic for Puritans. When Jesus' mother told him, "They have no wine," he didn't answer, "Good; they ought to be drinking lemonade!" No, he poured wine, and he poured it in abundance. He left the wedding feast a wedding feast, but he transformed it.

Christian business will be characterized by excellence—and by love. Christian education will teach people to think—and to think about God. Christian politics will promote the common good of people on earth—and it will be the true good of all. Christian recreation will re-create—and the unannounced presence of Jesus will inebriate people with something other than wine.

When the bishops at Vatican II wanted to "explain to everyone" how they, as members of the Council, understood the presence and activity of the Church in the world of today, they began with the sentence:

> The joys and hopes, the griefs and the anxieties
> of the people of this age, especially those who
> are poor or in any way afflicted, these too are
> the joys and hopes, the griefs and anxieties of
> the followers of Christ. Indeed, nothing
> genuinely human fails to raise an echo in their
> hearts, for [the Church] is a community of
> human beings.[1]

This sounds much like the way Jesus presented himself to the citizens of his hometown: "He has sent me to bring good news to the poor, to proclaim liberty to captives and recovery of sight to the blind, to let the oppressed go free."

God's plan for the "fullness of time," Saint Paul tells us, is to "bring all things in the heavens and on earth into one under Christ's headship" (see Ephesians 1:9-10). Jesus did not come to polarize human life between "religious" and "secular" activities, between are "eternal" and "temporal" values, between concern for what is of this world and what belongs to the next. Rather, Jesus came to unify things, to unify our outlook and our goals, to bring together everything we do under one single, driving purpose in life: to establish the reign of God on earth. Jesus sends us to make everything better in family and social life, in business and politics, by bringing every area and activity of human life under the life-giving reign of Christ.

God knows the value of all we try to do on earth. He knows our needs. God instilled in us our human aspirations and desires. Jesus said, "Strive first for the kingdom of God and his righteousness"—in everything you do—"and all these things will be given to you as well."

This is purity of heart, single-mindedness, religion without religiosity. It is what it means to be a steward of the kingship of Christ.

The Commitment to Stewardship

The question is, do I want to be a part of this effort? Do I want to dedicate myself, my life, to establishing the reign of God on earth?

The point to notice here is that this is not a matter of changing jobs or of taking time from what I do in order to do something else. The reign of God is not established through projects or by taking on extra "apostolic activities." Rather, we make every activity we engage in apostolic. We establish God's reign by doing what we are already doing, but by doing it with only one purpose in mind: to bring everything in heaven and on earth together into harmony under Christ's headship.

The key word is responsibility. A steward is someone who is responsible. The steward is not just a worker; the steward is in charge; the steward has to answer for what is done and not done. That is what responsibility means.

When we were made one with Jesus at Baptism we became responsible for bringing everything on earth under the reign of God. We are responsible for everything. We are not department heads or sub-managers. We share in the kingship of Christ himself. We are stewards of Christ the King. We are responsible for everything he is responsible for. If we drive through substandard housing on our way to work, we recognize that we have a responsibility to do what we can to change it. Substandard housing does not belong in the kingdom of God.

If we see a beer can on the street we are responsible for picking it up. If someone threw a beer can into our backyard, we would pick it up. The street is our Father's backyard. But being responsible for everything does not mean we have to do everything ourselves. That is manifestly impossible. If we tried to pick up all the beer cans on the street we wouldn't have time for anything else and we would neglect other, more important things for which we are responsible. We have to decide prudently how to use our time. We have to be selective. We take responsibility for making prudent choices.

The manager of a store is responsible for everything in it. If one day the manager walked into the store and saw in one glance a man shoplifting an article off the shelf, a lady fainting in the aisle, a light bulb that had burnt out and a wall that needed painting, the first thing that manager would have to do is make a choice. In emergency rooms they call it "triage."

The manager in this example would probably help the fainting lady first while shouting to a security guard to pick up the shoplifter. Next in priority might be the light bulb, while conceivably the wall might never get painted at all. If a supervisor came and asked about the wall, the manager would be responsible—would have to answer for it. But the manager's answer might well be, "I know the wall needs painting. Right now I don't have the time or the money to get it done. I'll see what I can do about it later."

That would be a responsible answer. A manager is responsible for everything. But a manager cannot do everything personally. To be responsible we have to make prudent choices about what we are actually able to do.

As managers or stewards of the kingship of Christ, we accept responsibility for renewing everything on earth. But we cannot do it all ourselves. So we make prudent judgments about how and where to invest our time and energies, and we pray for everything we see but cannot do. We consider ourselves involved in everything other people are doing to establish the reign of God on earth. Everyone's effort is our effort, everyone's cause is our cause, so long as it is moving in the direction of the fulfillment desired by God. Jesus said, "Whoever is not against you is for you" (Luke 9:50). As stewards of Christ's kingship, we accept and we proclaim solidarity with all the legitimate strivings of the human race. We support them as much as we can. We acknowledge our special solidarity with all who are consciously the body of Christ throughout the world. We share with them the explicit mission of establishing the reign of God on earth. To accept this involvement is stewardship.

The Fifth Grave: Dying to Despair

The greatest obstacle to involving ourselves in efforts to transform the world is a combined sense of hopelessness and helplessness.

"It's useless. Nothing can be done. You can't change anything."

"There's nothing I can do about it. Who am I? I don't have any authority to change things. Who's going to listen to me?"

Frustration is hard to deal with. So we anesthetize ourselves with indifference. We pass from, "There's nothing I can do about it" to "I'm not going to get involved" to "It doesn't concern me."

We cop out, psychologically as well as physically. We refuse to think about what is happening, or about how things ought to be, compared to how they are. We withdraw into isolationism. We mind our own business, we look after ourselves.

For some this isolationism takes the form of

absorption in the goals of this world: financial security, advancement, achievement—anything we think we
might actually succeed at; anything we can do by the
law of cause and effect working through our human
powers; anything that gives us a sense of accomplish-
ment.

We isolate ourselves from the big picture of God's
plan for us because we feel frustrated. We absorb ourselves instead in the small picture of our own more
manageable plans for ourselves. Soon we find ourselves compulsively doing what we can do, without
stopping to ask whether this is what we ought to do or
even what we really want to do.

For others, isolationism takes the form of
escapism. This is a more radical despair. Our chief preoccupation in life becomes avoiding all the challenges
we can. We withdraw, every chance we get, into the
imaginary world of entertainment and play.

Withdrawal from the world can take many forms.
Excessive drinking is one, and we recognize this as a
loss of freedom, as a compulsion. But in a sense all
chronic escapism is compulsive. TV can be a compulsion. Going out can be a compulsion. Golf or working
at a hobby can be a compulsion if we do it not just to
get a break and to get our minds off things for a while,
but as a means to avoid something we ought to be con-
fronting, as a means to take our minds off life itself.
Compulsive withdrawal can be all-absorbing; it can
keep us from experiencing anything else. It can blind
us to life as it is, not only in its ugliness but also in its
glory and promise.

All chronic escapism is an escape from the work of the kingdom. When we find ourselves taking every chance we can to get away from what is around us; when we notice that we don't ever think about the deep challenges any more, not even about those that go with our jobs; when we always choose to stay home and watch TV instead of going to a lecture, a discussion, a retreat, we need to ask ourselves some questions. We might have a responsibility problem as stewards of the kingship of Christ.

False Power, False Powerlessness

Jesus spoke about both power and powerlessness as ways of closing our eyes to the whole picture. To narrow our focus to success for its own sake is bad stewardship, and it drives us to blind escapism.

After praising the "the faithful and prudent servant, whom the master...will find at work when he arrives," Jesus speaks by contrast of the unfaithful steward who begins to wonder if the master is ever coming back (see Matthew 24:45-51). The unfaithful steward stops thinking about the master's return, stops thinking about pleasing the master at all as the reason and focus of his own job, and begins instead "to beat his fellow servants, and eat and drink with drunkards."

First, the bad manager uses power and authority abusively to get things done ("to beat his fellow servants"). There is no business in life but business, and its only law is profit. People and personal goals are sacrificed on the altar of advancement. Job satisfaction is sacrificed to productivity, quality service is sacrificed to short-term profits. We see it happening every day.

This is despair of real power expressing itself through absorption in limited power. Like the man who copes with helplessness on the job by going home and abusing his wife, we put all our energies into doing what we can as a way of forgetting what we cannot do.

As a result of abusing power, the unfaithful steward begins "to eat and drink with drunkards." When love is no longer our motivation, when pleasing the master has ceased to be our focus, it is hard to live with what is left. There is no way we can abuse others without subsequently abusing ourselves to escape from it. The abuse of power makes us powerless against the demons tormenting our soul. There is no escape except to "eat and drink," and to do so with others who are as intoxicated with illusion as we are, until we sink deeper and deeper into the stupor of a deadened mind and heart.

When imposed powerlessness frustrates us, we distract ourselves with chosen powerlessness. Like alcoholics who make drinking their problem rather than face the problem that drives them to drink, we give up control over our appetites so that this particular powerlessness will be our focus rather than the more frightening powerlessness we experience over our lives as such.

Because we feel the car is out of control we take our hands off the wheel and shut our eyes while our life goes over the cliff. This doesn't have to take the form of something obvious like alcoholism; it can be simply a matter of closing our eyes to the problems around us and refusing to take any responsibility for solving them. In spite of his wife's complaints, a husband refuses to see any problem in their marriage. A mother closes her eyes to signs of sexual abuse in her children. An employee chooses not to take a hard look at destructive policies and practices at the work-site. A priest won't listen to what might be wrong with his ministry in the parish.

Whether our sense of frustration and despair hides itself under the use of power or the abdication of power, we are refusing to take responsibility for the reign of God. And the root of our problem, if it is not just selfishness, is our failure to believe in the presence and power of Christ.

The Apparent Absence of God

Part of the common Christian experience is a keen awareness of the absence of God. It is not that God is really absent. It is just that we do not see him, frequently do not feel his presence and cannot understand why he isn't doing more than he seems to be doing to overcome evil in the world.

The Gospels are full of the theme of Christ's leaving. When, after he had multiplied bread in the wilderness, the people wanted to make him their king, Jesus "withdrew again to the mountain alone." In a preview of his ascension into heaven, he left his disciples alone in their boat (symbol of the Church), rowing against the wind and the waves in a contrary sea (see Matthew 14:22-33; John 6:1-22).

This is the typical experience of Christian life on earth. The Church is "battered by the waves"—especially those members of the Church who are trying to establish the reign of God in the frequently hostile environments of business and social life, family life and politics. Jesus does not appear to be in the boat. The "wind is against them" and they are "far from land."

Then Jesus comes, walking across the sea, and they are terrified. They are not sure it is he. They think he is a ghost. They aren't really certain until Peter risks his life by jumping into the stormy waves, believing he can walk on the water!

This is what stewardship means: working to establish the reign of God in a world where the winds and currents of culture are frequently against the values Christ teaches—and trying to do this without any perceptible help from Jesus, at least for much of the time.

When Jesus does come, in the form of a suggestion, an idea, an inspiration, our first reaction is terror. The risk is too great. There isn't the ghost of a chance. Does God think we can walk on water? You never really know whether God is calling you until you answer. Jesus only calls those to walk on the water who are willing to jump in, even at the risk of drowning.

The steward is someone left in charge while the master is "away on a journey." The steward is charged with responsibility for the kingdom and is to be intent on the master's business until he comes again. The steward may feel abandoned and alone when the master is not there. But regardless, the steward has to take full responsibility, make decisions, take decisive action, initiate changes and reforms and persevere in doing this until the master returns.

'Take Courage; I Have Conquered the World'

In order to persevere, we need hope, a hope based on faith. The steward has to believe not only that the master will return, but that he will return in triumph, that he has "conquered the world" (John 16:33).

To be faithful stewards of the reign of Christ, we have to believe that the war is already won, and we are just fighting the battles. We may win or lose this particular engagement, but fighting it is our contribution to the overall victory of God.

To use an image more consistent with Christ's refusal to impose his reign by force, we are like players in a basketball game who are losing 104 to 0. The coach calls us over and says, "Get out there and play your hearts out. We can win this game!"

We look up at the time clock. The coach has covered it with a cloth. If we go out on the court and play our hearts out until the whistle blows, we have faith. And we are showing it in action; that is fidelity. If we persevere in believing that Jesus will triumph, that is faith. If we persevere in working to bring about his triumph, that is fidelity.

We know in faith that Jesus is not absent. We know he is still present among us, living in our hearts, working in his Church, working in the heart of every human being who will listen even slightly to his voice. We know he is present, but we do not see him. We have to believe. We know he is working in us, with us, through us, but we do not see the results. We have to trust. We know he has triumphed over sin and evil, but everything we see around us contradicts this. We have to persevere in faith, in hope and in the love that keeps us working and spending our lives for him until he comes.

To be a steward of the kingship of Christ means persevering in faith and fidelity until he comes. For those whose focus remains fixed on Christ while they promote his reign, belief in the master's return is a sustaining hope. We know the truth: Jesus has overcome the world. He will "come again in glory to judge the living and the dead, and his kingdom will have no end." That kingdom is what we are creating now.

Die to Despair; Rise to Perseverance

The fifth and last grave we have to enter is the grave of dying to hopelessness. We have to refuse absolutely to judge by appearances, to believe that nothing is getting better, that nothing can get better. We have to take our reliance on human efforts down into the grave and rise with reliance on the power of God— which launches us into greater human efforts than before.

We do not look at what is happening around us to see whether Jesus has overcome the world. As Christians we believe that Jesus *has* overcome the world and look around us to see how it is happening—or how we can make it happen by getting involved. We commit ourselves to work for the transformation of the world.

This transformation begins with doing what we can to change our own environments. We fill our family life with the "fruit of the Spirit": love, joy, peace, patient endurance, kindness, generosity, faithfulness, gentleness and self-control. We try to fill our social life with the values of Christ, to make everything we do for entertainment rebuild us—to make recreation truly recreative. We use physical things to give joy to our hearts; we interact with other people in ways that bring us closer to them in mind and heart and soul.

In our professional environment, our job, school or business, we work to establish a tone of peace and respect, of true service to others. We encourage policies that transform work into love. We strive to make working an experience of giving. We keep our hearts alive by feeding them all day with the life-giving fire of generosity and helpfulness. We are willing to take a second look at goals and objectives, at ends and means, and we invite others to look at them as well. We ask how policies can be improved in the light of deeper human needs. We broaden our perspective, asking how we can do more to enhance our lives and the lives of others through what we already do, through what we are trained and committed to do.

We take ownership in our city, our neighborhood, our country, our state. We look at how other people and groups are transforming society, sometimes with the best of intentions, sometimes with the worst. We listen for an authentic voice of truth—not for a voice that tries to impose the faith of Christians on others, but for a voice that urges truth in the name of truth, love in the name of love, peace in the name of peace. The voice of truth speaks in the language of this world, proposing a way that is based on truth and leads to life, and we join our voices to it.

We discern such a voice by its conformity with the way in which we hope, the truth in which we believe, the life that has led us into love. Where no such voice is raised, we lift up our own, even when we seem to be a voice crying in the wilderness.

We rise from the grave of hopelessness to take on stewardship, to assume responsibility for establishing the life-giving reign of Christ over every area and activity of human existence. We pledge ourselves to persevere in faith and fidelity, to work faithfully until he comes.

This is the fifth and final step. Taken together with the others it brings us into the fullness of life.

Questions for Reflection and Discussion

- *What did I become responsible for when I was anointed at Baptism as a steward of Christ's kingship? How am I living up to this responsibility?*

- *What do I see around me that is not submitted to the reign of Christ—in business? in politics? in social life? in the media? in politics? in my family life? What is the difference between bringing authentic religion into these areas, or just bringing simplistic religiosity?*

- *What reason do I have to believe that Jesus has triumphed over the power of sin in these areas? Does my belief give me enough hope to try to change things?*

- *In what concrete and specific ways can I take responsibility for transforming the world as a steward of the kingship of Christ? How, when, where will I do this?*

Notes

[1] *Pastoral Constitution on the Church in the Modern World (Gaudium et Spes)*, adapted from Walter Abbot's translation, *The Documents of Vatican II* (America Press, 1966), p. 198.

Conclusion

---■---

Five Words in Series

The only way to get anywhere is to start from where you are. Each of these steps—except the first one, of course—presupposes the one before it. If you start school with the eighth grade without going through the other grades, you're bound to get confused.

Suppose, for example, someone began with the fifth commitment—to transform society as a steward of Christ's kingship—without having made the other four steps. What would happen?

More than likely, that person would end up acting

out of anger, polarizing people and resorting to violence. Those who work for peace and justice know that peace must take priority in their own hearts or they will accomplish nothing. The axiom, "There is no peace without justice" cuts both ways: Authentic Christian justice can be brought only about through peace.

A bishop in Guatemala told me, "Any government which establishes itself through violence will have to sustain itself through violence." The same is true of any peace, any settlement, any working arrangement between people that is brought about by pressure, intimidation or fear.

The lesson of Jesus is that love conquers the world. If we conquer by any other power, it is we who have been defeated. This means I cannot take on the commitment to transform the world as a steward of Christ's kingship until I have surrendered myself to die for the world in love as a victim of Christ's priesthood.

The victim Jesus offered as priest was himself: his body, his flesh for the life of the world. As "priests in the Priest" we have no other victim to offer but the one he offered: his body, which we are. There is no other way to establish the kingdom except the way of the cross and that is a way of all-enduring love.

Before we can accept the "sending"—the "apostolate"—of Jesus, we have to accept his Spirit: the Spirit of love, unity and peace. The starting-point of all apostolates is the upper room, the place of community, where all "devoted themselves with one accord to prayer" (Acts 1:14). Only out of the deep, communal peace and surrender of this upper room can Christians go out to transform the world.

How do we get to this surrender?

Evangelization

We begin by entering into the first grave, the act of life-giving despair, which grounds us in the deep realization that we will never do anything that is worthy of what we are unless we do it with Jesus. When we truly believe in him as the only possible savior of our lives in this world, we will commit ourselves to making interaction with him the saving guidance and power in everything we do.

Discipleship

This naturally leads us to discipleship. We interact with Jesus by learning from him. We cannot walk by the light unless we see by the light, and this means opening our minds to the teaching and example of Jesus. It means committing time to reflection and prayer.

But what makes us able to persevere in discipleship? People constantly make resolutions to pray more, to read Scripture, to give time to meditation or to group discussions. Most of these resolutions don't last long. Why can't we, or why don't we, live up to our commitments to lead a life of discipleship?

The first reason is that we haven't really made the first step deeply enough. We are not really convinced that interaction with Jesus is a necessity, not an extra, in our lives. We haven't despaired enough of every-thing else to hope entirely in him. We think we can get along—at least in some areas of our lives—without actively, explicitly involving him.

Or we haven't entered into the second grave com-pletely. We are not totally convinced that the goals and guidance of this world are inadequate. We think we know enough, or can learn enough from what is avail-able in the culture, to live happy and productive lives. We don't think we really have to be disciples. And so we don't give first priority to learning the message and way of Jesus.

Or we think we have "already learned our reli-gion." We think that through the laws and instruction we have received we have absorbed the Light of the world. We choose legalism over discipleship.

But if we really make the second step, if we begin to study at the feet of Jesus and to live lives character-ized by reflection on his words and example, we nat-urally pass to the third step. We begin to see how the gospel applies to life. We begin to see how we can live out the teaching of Jesus in new, creative, innovative ways. We gain prophetic insights.

Witness

But we might fail to act on what we see. Many do. As Jesus himself pointed out, the seed that has broken through the beaten path of culture, that has put down roots through discipleship and has begun to grow, can still be choked out and strangled by "worldly anxiety and the lure of riches" (Matthew 13:22). We begin to see the radical choices to which the gospel invites us. But we also sense what they will cost. We realize what we may have to give up, what we may lose.

At this point, if we had the support of the whole Christian community, if all the people we are close to were united in making the same radical choices we see, we would go along. There is a sense of safety in numbers. We would rather give up what we enjoy than give up our close relationships with others. It is sometimes easier to follow the crowd than to be left behind, even when the crowd is headed for martyrdom.

But it is hard to stand alone. To be a prophet, then, we have to enter into the third grave; we have to die to our fear of standing alone. We have to be willing to make radical choices, to take frightening risks, even when no one supports us. We have to listen to the Spirit in our hearts, confirm what we feel moved to do by checking its conformity with the word of God— and, in more serious choices, consult a spiritual director who can discern with us on the level of the Spirit's inspirations rather than just on the level of cultural common sense. Finally, we have to have the courage to stand up "in solitary witness"[1] as a prophet of Jesus Christ.

The Danger of Pride. To be a prophet is a dangerous thing—not only for the body, but for the soul. When those who have the courage to stand up in solitary witness look around and see that they are the only ones standing, they begin to realize that they are the only ones who are right—at least about this particular issue. From this comes the danger of pride.

Pride does not mean thinking you are better than others; that is just vanity, conceit, an error in judgment, stupidity. It is not such a serious sin. But if we are right often enough, we may conclude we are smart. There is no sin in that either; it may simply be the truth. If we ever decide, however, that because we are smart, then whatever we think must be true, that is the sin of making ourselves the standard of truth and falsity. And that is pride. Real pride means seeing oneself as the criterion, the standard, of truth and falsity, of good and evil. This is the sin of sins. Only God is the criterion.

Prophets are in danger of taking themselves too seriously, especially when other people do. After all, you cannot be a prophet without attracting notice. People who come out of the desert like John the Baptizer, wearing camel's hair jumpsuits and eating bugs, tend to draw a crowd. Your enemies can't even stone you to death without making you the center of attention!

The Danger of Alienation. The crowd that gathers around prophets is often a hostile crowd. Prophets can be threatening. Even if you are not trying to persuade someone to follow your religious beliefs, even if all you want to do is live the gospel authentically in your own life, your example will be a threat to others. Acts of Christian witness have a way of summoning people to search their own souls, whether they want to or not.

So prophets tend to get stoned, and this can lead the prophet into anger and bitterness. Stones hurt. Rejection hurts. Being taken for wrong when you are right hurts. The prophet is in danger of being swallowed up by anger and bitterness.

By the fact of standing alone, the prophet tends to be alienated from community. To be different in any way is already in some measure to put oneself on the outside of the crowd. To be attacked and rejected increases the distance.

We mustn't give up being prophets or lessen the radical nature of our prophetic stance, but we cannot remain mere prophets either. We have to go on to be priests. And this means entering into a fourth grave: We have to die to "rugged individualism" in religion, to any attachment we have to keeping our religion an individual, private affair between ourselves and God.

Community

To be prophets we have to be willing to stand alone. To be priests we have to die to the limitations of this solitary stance. We have to involve ourselves with others. Our expression of faith must become an expression of love. The faith we express before others as prophets we have to express with others as priests. The goal of our self-expression as priests is not just authenticity; it is ministry. We give expression to the light and love within us in order to nurture and mediate God's divine life to others.

To be priest is to enter into community. It is to form

community. The priest's expression of faith, hope and love is intended to draw people into the communion of the Holy Spirit by giving them a deeply felt experience of the grace of our Lord Jesus Christ and of the love of God.

The priest is by definition a nurturer. The priest's focus is on mediating the light, love and life of God to others, on drawing people into the life-giving community of redeemed humanity. The priest's focus is on bringing about unity and peace.

The prophet, on the other hand, is primarily focused on authenticity, on living out the truth, regardless of consequences. The prophet "lays the ax to the root of the tree" (see Matthew 3:10) and lets the chips fall where they will.

Jesus was speaking of himself as prophet when he said, "Do you think that I have come to establish peace upon the earth? No, I tell you, but rather division. ...[A] father will be divided against his son and a son against his father, a mother against her daughter and a daughter against her mother, a mother-in-law against her daughter-in-law and a daughter-in-law against her mother-in-law" (Luke 12:51-53).

Jesus was speaking as priest when he said at the Last Supper, "I pray for...the ones you have given me...that they may all be one, as you, Father, are in me and I in you...that they may be one, as we are one...that they may be brought to perfection as one...that the love with which you loved me may be in them and I in them" (see John 17:9-26).

These two statements are not contradictory. Most

of the practical problems in Christianity are solved by thinking in terms of "both...and" rather than "either... or."

Priest and prophet are like oil and vinegar: You have to have both to make salad dressing. Vinegar alone is too harsh; so is prophetic witness. Oil alone is too bland; so is priestly ministry that does not challenge. Being pure vinegar can alienate one from the community. Being pure oil can make one nothing but a facilitator of what the community already wants to do—a pleaser, someone afraid to make waves. In Jesus the most compassionate, self-giving love the world had ever seen was joined to the most radical witness the world had ever seen. Jesus was Prophet and Priest.

We have to be priests as well as prophets. But we also have to be prophets before we are priests. If we have never had the courage to stand alone, to take an unpopular stance, to risk arousing hostility in others, how will we ever know whether our choice to "temper the wind to the shorn lamb," to moderate our position out of compassion for people's woundedness, is really an act of giving priority to love or just a fear of conflict?

Apostolate

We can't stop with priesthood either. If we did the Christian community would run the risk of being just a warm, nurturing womb of love entirely turned in on itself while the world goes to hell in a handbasket.

We have to take responsibility for the world, for

those around us, for the human race. We have to dedicate ourselves to transforming society, to changing social structures, to working for peace on earth, to extending the reign of Christ over every area and activity of human life.

For this we have authority. We have a right that is ours, as every right is, by virtue of an obligation. We transform society in obedience to the command of him who said, "All power in heaven and on earth has been given to me. Go, therefore, and make disciples of all nations..." (see Matthew 28:18-20).

As we have seen, "all nations" doesn't mean just all geographical entities; it means all areas, all fields of human life and activity. And to "make disciples... teaching them to observe all that I have commanded you" doesn't mean just to catechize; it means to instill the attitudes and values taught by Jesus, and the policies that follow from these, into the social structures of every institution and society on earth. It means to renew society, not simplistically, but with respect for the aspirations and goals of the human race created and redeemed by God.

The paradox is that to renew society as stewards of Christ's kingship, to establish the reign of God as Jesus gave himself to establish it, we have to die to seeing it happen. We have to be willing to persevere in faith and fidelity unconditionally, whether or not we see any results, until Christ comes again, whenever that might be.

Jesus won his victory in the act of accepting defeat on the cross. The supreme triumph of his power was his renunciation of power. He revealed the true nature of power by refusing to triumph except through human powerlessness. He won life for the world by accepting death on the cross.

When we are ready to die with him as priests, we will be ready to conquer the world for him as stewards of his kingship. We don't have to wait until we are perfect to begin, but we have to begin at the beginning.

If you want to enter into the fullness of life, now is the time to start. Go back to page one of this book and begin reading it again, pausing as long as is necessary to make decisions as you go. Better yet, get someone else to read it with you so that you can help each other to understand, to decide and to act.

Jesus came that we might "have life, and have it to the full." The fullness of life is yours, if you choose it. Jesus says, "Come, follow me." The way is open, if you choose to follow it. And the first steps are clear.

Do you choose to begin?

Notes

[1] This phrase is the title of a book by Gordon Zahn that tells the story of Franz Jaegerstaetter, a conscientious objector who was beheaded in Nazi Germany for refusing to fight in Hitler's army.